国际会计英语核心词汇

审计

双语名词与解析

杜　英◎主编

English-Chinese Explanations
for Auditing Terminology

上海财经大学出版社

图书在版编目(CIP)数据

审计双语名词与解析 / 杜英主编 . —上海：上海财经大学出版社，2017. 7

ISBN 978 - 7 - 5642 - 2627 - 5/F.2627

Ⅰ. ①审… Ⅱ. ①杜… Ⅲ. ①审计—名词—词汇—汉、英 Ⅳ. ①F239

中国版本图书馆 CIP 数据核字(2017)第 192033 号

□ 责任编辑 吴晓群
□ 封面设计 张克瑶

SHENJI SHUANGYU MINGCI YU JIEXI

审 计 双 语 名 词 与 解 析

杜 英 主编

上海财经大学出版社出版发行
(上海市中山北一路 369 号 邮编 200083)
网 址：http://www.sufep.com
电子邮箱：webmaster @ sufep.com
全国新华书店经销
上海华教印务有限公司印刷装订
2017 年 7 月第 1 版 2017 年 7 月第 1 次印刷

890mm×1240mm 1/32 4.125 印张(插页：1) 100 千字
印数：0001—2000 定价：45.00 元

Foreword / 前言

在经济全球化的今天,财经人才面临的要求不断地在提高,具有国际执业资格的财会人员将更具有市场竞争力。近二十年来,一些国际知名的职业会计师团体逐渐进入中国市场,英国ACCA、加拿大CPA、澳大利亚CPA、美国AICPA等执业资格考试对我国的财会从业人员来说,已经不再是不可逾越的障碍。越来越多的中国大学生以及财经界的在职人员加入了国际执业资格考试的大军。

审计是财经类专业的一门基础学科,在上述所有的资格考试中,审计都是必考科目。它具有突出的实践性,但在其学科性质上又具有一定的理论性和抽象性。从学习的目的而言,必须首先透彻理解其概念框架,其次才是运用概念框架解决实际问题。缺乏对基本概念和原理的了解,我们的学习就会困难重重。但是,对于中国人而言,如何快速理解这些英文专业术语,将是一项巨大的挑战。

作为一名从事审计双语教学超过二十年的专业教师,笔者对于中国学生在学习英文版的审计教材时面临的问题以及存在的误区有相当深入的了解。在教学过程中,笔者不止一次想到,如果有这样一本双语辅导书，将这些深奥、抽象的概念，用学生易于理解的语言来阐述与分析，一定可以大大提高学生的学习效率和效果。这便是笔者编写本书的目的。除了尽力用更浅显的中文对这些英文术语进行解释以外，笔者还附加了一些说明性文字（在书中用仿宋体标识），以帮助学生更好地理解这些概念。除此以外，本书还把学生在学习审计中的一些误区进行了总结，以提问和回答的方式进行编排，希望能够为学生解惑。本书的内容安排，主要参照了英国 ACCA 考试大纲中对审计（F8）科目的相关要求，同时也适用于其他执业资格审计科目的考试。

限于水平，本书在安排和表述上可能不十分恰当，甚至可能出现错误，恳请读者批评指正！

编　者

2017 年 7 月

Contents / 目录

Part A

Audit Framework and Regulation / 审计框架和规范

A－1 The Concepts of Audit and Other Assurance Engagements / 审计和其他鉴证业务的概念

Assurance Engagement

An assurance engagement is one in which a practitioner expresses a conclusion designed to enhance the degree of confidence of the intended users other than the responsible party about the outcome of the evaluation or measurement of a subject matter against criteria. An assurance engagement performed by a practitioner will consist of the following elements：a three party relationship，a subject matter，suitable criteria，evidence and an assurance report.

Intended users are the person，persons or class of persons for whom the practitioner prepares the assurance report.

The responsible party is the party responsible for the underlying subject matter or subject matter information of the assurance engagement.

The practitioner is the individual providing professional services that will review the subject matter and provide the assurance.

鉴证业务

鉴证业务是指执业人员对鉴证对象信息提出结论，以增强除责任方之外的预期使用者对鉴证对象信息信任程度的业务。执业人员通过收集充分、适当的证据来评价某个鉴证对象是否在所有重大方面符合适当的标准，并出具鉴证报告，从而提高该鉴证对象信息的可信性。鉴证业务要素，是指鉴证业务的三方关系、鉴证对象、标准、证据和鉴证报告。

预期使用者是指预期将使用由执业人员编制的鉴证报告的所有人员。

责任方是指对鉴证对象或者鉴证对象信息负责的组织或人员。

执业人员是指提供专业服务的人员，他们将审核鉴证对象并提供保证。

A－2 External Audit / 外部审计

External Audit

The objective of an audit of financial statements is to enable the auditor to express an opinion on whether the financial statements are prepared, in all material respects, in accordance with an applicable financial reporting framework.

外部审计

财务报表审计的目标是审计人员在实施审计程序的基础上，

对财务报表是否在所有重大方面按照适用的财务报告框架编制发表意见。

Review Engagement

The objective of a review engagement is to enable a practitioner to state whether, on the basis of procedures which do not provide all the evidence that would be required in an audit, anything has come to the practitioner's attention that causes the practitioner to believe that the financial statements are not prepared, in all material respects, in accordance with an applicable financial reporting framework.

财务报表审阅

财务报表审阅的目标，是审计人员在实施审阅程序(其所需要提供的证据数量比审计程序所需要的证据数量少)的基础上，说明是否注意到某些事项，使其相信财务报表没有按照适用的财务报告框架的规定编制。

审阅程序比审计程序简单，以询问和分析程序为主，只有当有理由相信所审阅的财务报表可能存在重大错报时才需要追加其他程序。

【学习提示】

审计业务与审阅业务有什么区别?

鉴证业务包含审计业务和审阅业务以及其他鉴证业务。其中，执行审计业务需要遵循审计准则，执行审阅业务需要遵循审阅业务准则。审阅业务主要采用询问和分析程序获取证据，其所需证据的数量较少，检查风险较高，所以只能提供有限保证。

Reasonable Assurance

An audit gives the reader reasonable assurance on the truth and fairness of the financial statements, which is a high, but not absolute, level of assurance.

合理保证

由于审计固有的局限性，通过审计程序，审计人员只能对财务报表的真实性和公允性提供很高的但不是绝对的保证程度。

Limited Assurance

Limited assurance is a lower level of assurance. It allows for a lesser amount of testing and evaluation and results in a negative conclusion.

有限保证

有限保证是一种较低程度的保证。为了以消极方式提出结论，执业人员可以执行比较少的测试程序。

【学习提示】

如何区分合理保证与有限保证？

合理保证的鉴证业务的目标是审计人员将鉴证业务风险降至该业务环境下可接受的低水平，以此作为以积极方式发表意见的基础。例如，在历史财务信息审计中，要求审计人员将审计风险降至该业务环境下可接受的低水平，对审计后的历史财务信息提供高水平保证（合理保证），在审计报告中对历史财务信息采用积极方式提出结论。例如："我们认为，ABC公司财务报表在所有重大方面按照适当的财务报告框架（比如IFRS）的规定编制，公允反映了ABC公司20×1年12月31日的财务状况以及20×1年度的经营成果和现金流量。"

有限保证的鉴证业务的目标是审计人员将鉴证业务风险降至该业务环境下可接受的水平，以此作为以消极方式提出结论的基础。在历史财务信息审阅中，要求审计人员将审阅风险降至该业务环境下可接受的水平（可接受的审阅风险水平将高于可接受的审计风险），对审阅后的历史财务信息提供较低水平的保证（有限保证），在审阅报告中对历史财务信息采用消极方式提出结论。例如："根据我们的审阅，我们没有注意到任何事项使我们相信，ABC公司财务报表没有按照适当的财务报告框架的规定编制，未能在所有重大方面公允反映审阅单位的财务状况、经营成果和现金流量。"

True and Fair

True — Information is factual and conforms with reality in that there are no factual errors. In addition it is assumed that to be true, it must comply with accounting standards and any relevant legislation. Lastly, true includes data being correctly transferred from accounting records to the financial statements.

Fair — Information is clear, impartial and unbiased, and also reflects plainly the commercial substance of the transactions of the entity.

真实与公允

真实是指会计信息应如实反映事实及现行状况，不存在对事实的错报。会计信息除了被认为是真实的外，还必须遵守会计准则和相关的法规。另外，真实性还包括将会计记录的内容如实地反映在财务报表中。

公允是指会计信息是清晰的、公正的和不偏不倚的，并且准确地反映企业交易活动的商业实质。

A－3 Corporate Governance / 公司治理

Corporate Governance

Corporate governance is the system by which companies are directed and controlled. Corporate governance considers the responsibilities of directors, how the board of directors should be run and structured, the need for good internal controls and the relationship with external auditors.

公司治理

公司治理是指企业指挥和控制的系统。公司治理主要涉及董事的责任，以及董事会的组织和运作，对良好的内部控制的需要以及与外部审计的关系。

Those Charged with Governance

Those charged with governance are the person(s) or organization(s) (e.g., a corporate trustee) with responsibility for overseeing the strategic direction of the entity and obligations related to the accountability of the entity. This includes overseeing the financial reporting process. For some entities in some jurisdictions, those charged with governance may include management personnel.

治理层

治理层是指对被审计单位战略方向以及管理层履行经营管理责任负有监督责任的人员或组织（比如公司的受托人）。治理层的责任包括对财务报告过程的监督。治理层一般是指董事会，包括执行董事和非执行董事。在某些情况下，治理层也包括管理层的成员。

Management

Management refers to the person(s) or organization(s) with executivc responsibility for the conduct of the entity's operations. For some entities in some jurisdictions, management includes some or all of those charged with governance, for example, executive members of a governance board, or an owner-manager.

管理层

管理层是指对被审计单位经营活动的执行负有管理责任的人员或组织。管理层一般包括企业的经理和其他高级管理人员，如总经理(CEO)、财务总监(CFO)等。在某些情况下，公司管理层包括部分或全部治理层的成员，比如，治理委员会中的执行成员或者业主经理。管理层负责编制财务报表，并受治理层的监督。在实务中，治理层成员与管理层成员往往存在交叉的现象。例如，董事长兼任总经理，董事兼任总经理或其他高级管理职务等。

OECD Principles of Corporate Governance

The OECD (Organization for Economic Cooperation and Development) principles of corporate governance set out the rights of shareholders, the importance of disclosure and transparency and the responsibilities of the board of directors.

OECD 公司治理的基本原则

OECD(经济合作与发展组织,简称经合组织)公司治理的基本原则明确了股东的责任、信息披露和透明的重要性,以及董事会的职责。

Principles of the UK Corporate Governance Code

The UK Corporate Governance Code, produced by the FRC, sets out standards of good practice regarding board leadership and effectiveness, accountability (including audit), remuneration and relations with shareholders.

英国公司治理准则

英国公司治理准则(原称 Combined Code),由英国财务报告委员会(FRC)发布,为良好的公司治理实务设立了标准,主要内容包括董事会的领导力、有效性、责任(包括审计)、薪酬以及与股东的关系。

【学习提示】

英国公司治理准则的主要内容是什么?

在分析一家企业的公司治理结构是否符合公司治理的基本原则时,我们经常以英国公司治理准则为标准。其基本要求中值得我们关注的内容主要如下：

1. 有关“领导力”的规定，主要包括：

(1) 两职分离。董事长(Chairman)与总经理(CEO)应当分别由不同的人员担任，实行两职分离。董事长主要负责管理董事会，而总经理主要负责管理公司的经营。

(2) 除了执行董事外，董事会内部还应当包含非执行董事，并且非执行董事与执行董事的人数应当基本相等，这样才能保证非执行董事在董事会中发挥积极的作用。

2. 有关“有效性”的规定，主要包括：

(1) 为了有效履行他们的职责，董事会以及各委员会应当具备相应的技能、经验，并且要及时更新自己的知识结构。

(2) 应当有一个正式、严格、透明的评估机制来评价整个董事会及其成员的业绩。

(3) 应当定期选举新董事。

(4) 新董事的任命应当有一个严格、透明、正式的程序。

3. 关于责任，公司治理准则中指出：

(1) 董事会应当对公司的现状和前景进行不偏不倚和简明易懂的评价。

(2) 董事会有责任确定为实现战略目标将要承担的风险，并且应当建立和维护健全的风险管理和内部控制系统。

(3) 董事会应当建立正式和透明的安排，以更好地运用公司报告和风险管理以及内部控制原理；董事会应当与公司的审计人员保持适当的联系。

4. 关于薪酬的要求，主要包括：

(1) 执行董事的薪酬安排应当能够促进公司的长远发展。薪酬中与业绩挂钩的元素应当透明、有弹性，并且一旦确定就要严格执行。

(2) 没有任何董事可以决定他们自己的薪酬。

5. 关于与股东的关系，准则要求：

董事会与股东之间应当积极对话，以便双方互相理解。董事会应当充分运用年度股东大会(AGM)与机构投资者沟通，并且鼓励他们参与。

OECD 公司治理的基本原则构建了一个良好的公司治理结构框架，各国在制定公司治理相关规则时大多参考了这些基本原则，并在此基础上加以细化，使其更具有可操作性。英国财务报告委员会(FRC)发布的英国公司治理准则则成为所有在伦敦交易所上市的公司的最佳实务准则。我们应该对这份准则有详细的了解，以此为标准来评价一家企业的公司治理结构是否存在问题，并提出改进建议。

Non-executive Directors

Non-executive directors are directors who do not have day-to-day responsibilities for the company. They are not employees of the company or affiliated with it in any other way.

非执行董事

非执行董事是公司的董事，但在其被委任的公司里没有日常经营管理上的责任。他们不是公司的员工，与公司也没有其他附属关系。

【学习提示】

非执行董事到底是什么人？

执行董事与非执行董事是相对的。所谓执行董事，其本身作为一个董事参与企业的经营，一般是公司内部人士，执行业务，从事内部的经营管理，但容易受环境限制，易因自身利益而忽视公司的长远利益。而非执行董事则与公司没有任何关系，可以独立发表自己的观点，对公司董事会的决策包括一些重大的问题独立发表意见。公司外聘的非执行董事大多是经济、法律、金融或人事管理方面的专门人才或是其他在政府或民间有发言权或有一定影响的人士，他们并不在公司中任职。

Audit Committee

An audit committee is a sub-committee of the board of directors, usually containing a number of non-executive directors.

审计委员会

审计委员会是董事会内设的一个主要由非执行董事组成的专业委员会。其目的是监督公司的会计、财务报告以及公司会计报表的审计。一般而言，审计委员会里至少要有3名非执行董事，其中至少有一名是财务专家。

如果审计委员会运行有效，就能够为公司带来巨大的效益：

1. 代表董事会审核财务报表，以此提高财务报告的质量；

2. 创造一个减少欺诈机会的纪律和控制氛围；

3. 使非执行董事能够给出独立的判断，并在企业经营控制中扮演积极的角色；

4. 帮助财务董事，使财务董事有机会可以提出他们所关注的问题；

5. 为外部审计人员提供沟通的渠道，从而加强外部审计人员的地位；

6. 当外部审计人员与公司管理人员发生争执时，为外部审计人员提供一个保持独立性的体制；

7. 向内部审计人员提供独立于管理人员的较大的独立性，强化内部审计职能的地位；

8. 增强公众对财务报表可靠性和客观性的信心。

【学习提示】

董事会中除审计委员会之外，还有其他委员会吗？

除了审计委员会，董事会还可以设立其他专业委员会，如薪酬委员会、提名委员会、风险委员会。薪酬委员的职责是确定执行董事的薪酬，提名委员负责执行董事的提名。薪酬委员会和提名委员会都由非执行董事组成。成立风险委员会的目的是帮助企业评估风险以及管理风险。

A－4 Professional Ethics / 职业道德

Fundamental Principles of Professional Ethics

Integrity: Members shall be honest and straightforward in all professional and business relationship.

Objectivity: Members shall be fair and not allow personal bias, conflict of interest or influence of others to override professional or business judgements.

Professional Competence and Due Care: Members have a continuing duty to maintain professional knowledge and skill at the level required to ensure that a client or employer receives competent professional services based on current development in practice, legislation and techniques; Members shall act diligently and in accordance with applicable technical and professional standards.

Confidentiality: Members shall respect the confidentiality of information acquired during the course of providing professional and business relationships and should not disclose any such information to third parties without proper and specific authority, or unless there is a legal or professional right or duty to disclose. Confidential information acquired as a result of professional and business relationships must not be used for the personal advantage of members or third parties.

Professional Behaviour: Members shall comply with relevant laws and regulations and avoid any action that discredits the profession.

职业道德基本原则

诚信: 会员在提供专业服务和商业服务时,应当保持正直和诚实。

客观: 会员应当公正处事、实事求是,不得由于偏见、利益冲突以及他人的不当影响而损害职业判断或商业判断。

专业胜任能力和应有的关注: 会员应当保持专业胜任能力,将专业知识和技能始终保持在应有的水平,跟上有关实务、法律法规和技术准则的最新发展,确保为客户提供具有专业水准的服务;会员应当勤勉尽责,按照有关技术和职业准则的要求,认真、全面、及时地完成工作任务。

保密: 会员应当对因职业关系和商业关系而获知的信息予以保密,未经客户授权或法律法规允许,不应当向会计师事务所以外的第三方披露其所获知的涉密信息。会员不可以利用因职业关系和商业关系而获知的涉密信息为自己或第三方谋取利益。

职业行为：会员应当遵守相关法律法规，避免发生任何有损职业声誉的行为。

【学习提示】

独立性原则是职业道德的基本原则吗?

上述五项基本原则（诚信、客观、专业胜任能力和应有的关注、保密、职业行为）构成了审计人员职业道德体系的基本框架。一定要注意，虽然独立性是我们经常提及的一项原则，但它并不是审计人员职业道德的基本原则。它之所以重要，是因为独立性是诚信和客观的基础。

Independence

Independence includes independence of mind and independence in appearance.

Independence of mind is that state of mind that permits the provision of an opinion without being affected by influences that compromise professional judgement, allowing an individual to act with integrity, and exercise objectivity and professional scepticism.

Independence in appearance: avoidance of facts and circumstances that are so significant that a reasonable and informed third party, having knowledge of all relevant information, including safeguards applied, would reasonably conclude a firm's, or a member of the assurance team's integrity, objectivity or professional scepticism had been comprised.

独立性

独立性包括实质上的独立性和形式上的独立性。独立性是指不受外来力量控制、支配,按照一定的规则行事。

实质上的独立性是一种内心状态,审计人员在提出结论时,不受损害职业判断的因素影响,诚信行事,遵循客观和公正原则,保持职业怀疑态度。

形式上的独立性是一种外在表现,审计人员应当回避那些事实和情况,而那些事实和情况会导致一个理性且掌握充分信息(包括所运用的防范措施)的第三方,合理推断会计师事务所或审计项目组成员损害了诚信原则、客观和公正原则或职业怀疑态度。

Threats to Independence and Objectivity

Threats to independence and objectivity may arise in the form of self-interest, self-review, advocacy, familiarity, and intimidation threats. Appropriate safeguards must be put in place to eliminate or reduce such threats to acceptable levels.

Self-interest Threat

A self-interest threat is that a financial or other interest will inappropriately influence the professional accountant's judgement or behaviour.

Self-review Threat

The self-review threat occurs when a previous judgement needs to be re-evaluated by members responsible for that judgement. The situation tends to arise when the auditor has provided other services to a client.

Advocacy Threat

The advocacy threat occurs when members promote a

position or opinion to the point that subsequent objectivity may be compromised.

Familiarity Threat

The familiarity threat occurs when, because of a close relationship, members become too sympathetic to the interest of others.

Intimidation Threat

The intimidation threat occurs when members are deterred from acting objectively by threats, actual or perceived.

对独立和客观产生不利影响的因素

可能对独立和客观产生不利影响的因素包括自身利益、自我评价、过度推介、密切关系和外在压力。审计人员应当采取适当的防范措施，以消除不利影响或者将其降低至可接受的水平。

自身利益导致的不利影响

如果经济利益或其他利益对会员的职业判断或行为产生不当影响，将产生自身利益导致的不利影响。

自身利益导致不利影响的情形主要包括：拥有客户的股票、接受客户的礼物和款待、或有收费以及会计师事务所的收入过分依赖某一客户等。

自我评价导致的不利影响

如果会员对其以前做出的判断进行再评价，将产生自我评价导致的不利影响。这种不利影响常常由于审计人员为自己的审计客户提供其他服务而产生。比如会计师事务所为客户编制会计报表，为客户提供内部审计服务、税务服务或者资产评估服务等。

过度推介导致的不利影响

如果会员过度推介客户或工作单位的某种立场或意见并使其

客观性受损害时，将产生过度推介导致的不利影响。

过度推介导致不利影响的情形主要包括：会计师事务所推介审计客户的股份；在审计客户与第三方发生诉讼或纠纷时，审计人员担任该客户的辩护人。

密切关系导致的不利影响

如果会员与客户或工作单位存在长期或亲密的关系，而过于倾向他们的利益，将产生密切关系导致的不利影响。

密切关系导致不利影响的情形主要包括：与客户存在长期业务关系；项目组成员与客户的董事、高级管理人员或所处职位能够对业务对象施加重大影响的员工有亲属关系或私人关系等。

外在压力导致的不利影响

如果会员受到实际的压力或因感受到压力而无法客观行事，将产生外在压力导致的不利影响。

外在压力导致的不利影响的情形主要包括：会计师事务所受到客户解除业务关系的威胁；客户威胁将起诉会计师事务所；会计师事务所受到降低收费的影响而不恰当地缩小工作范围等。

【学习提示】

如何应用职业道德的概念框架？

职业道德是审计学习的一个重点。我们应当学会应用职业道德的概念框架来解决相关问题。首先我们必须识别出对独立和客观产生不利影响的因素，然后评估这些不利影响的严重性，最后再判断采取何种防范措施来消除这些不利因素的影响。

Contingent Fees

Contingent fees are calculated on a predetermined basis relating to the outcome or result of a transaction or the result of the work performed.

或有收费

或有收费是指收费与否或收费多少取决于交易的结果或所执行工作的结果。比如会计师事务所的审计收费按照被审计单位是否能够取得银行贷款或者取得贷款的金额来收费，这样的安排就形成了一种或有收费。

会计师事务所在提供审计服务时，以直接或间接形式取得或有收费，将因自身利益产生非常严重的不利影响，导致没有防范措施能够将其降低至可接受的水平。除非法律法规有其他规定，否则会计师事务所不得采用这种收费安排。

Lowballing

When a firm quotes a significantly lower fee level for an audit service than would have been charged by the predecessor firm, there is a significant self-interest threat.

低价揽业

在审计人员承接业务时，如果其收费报价明显低于前任审计人员或其他会计事务所的相应报价，这也是自我利益产生的不利影响，因为这可能导致审计人员难以按照职业准则和相关的要求执行业务。这时，会计师事务所应当确保在提供专业服务时，遵守职业准则和相关的指南以及质量控制程序的要求，使工作质量不受损害。

Public Interest Entities

Public interest entities are defined as：

All listed entities；and Any entity：

(a) Defined by regulation or legislation as a public interest entity；or

(b) For which the audit is required by regulation or legislation to be conducted in compliance with the same independence requirements that apply to the audit of listed entities；and

(c) Entities that are of significant public interest because of their business，their size or their number of employees or their corporate status is such that they have a wide range of stakeholders.

公共利益实体

公共利益实体包括所有的上市公司和下列实体：

1. 法律法规界定的公共利益实体；

2. 法律法规规定按照上市公司审计独立性的要求接受审计的实体；

3. 其他具有重大公共利益的实体——因为它们的业务经营、企业规模、员工数量或者企业现状而导致其拥有数量众多且分布广泛的利益相关者。这样的实体包括信贷机构（比如银行）、保险公司、投资公司和养老金公司。

Key Audit Partner

The key audit partner may include：engagement partner；individual responsible for the engagement quality control review；or one of the other audit partners on the engagement team. The key audit partner makes key decisions or judgements on significant matters with respect to the audit of the financial statements on which the firm will express an opinion. Depending on the circumstances and the role of the individuals on the audit, "other audit partners" may include, for example, audit partners and responsible for significant subsidiaries or divisions.

关键审计合伙人

关键审计合伙人是指项目合伙人、实施项目质量控制复核的负责人,以及审计项目组中其他合伙人。关键审计合伙人负责对财务报表审计所涉及的重大事项做出关键决策或判断。根据特定情况或是在审计项目组中的作用,其他审计合伙人还可能包括负责审计重要子公司或分支机构的项目合伙人。

Preconditions for an Audit

Preconditions for an audit are the use by management of an acceptable financial reporting framework in the preparation of the financial statements and the agreement of management and, where appropriate, those charged with governance to the premise on which an audit is conducted.

执行审计工作的前提

执行审计工作的前提是:确定财务报告编制基础的可接受性;就管理层和治理层(如适用)的责任达成一致。

在确定财务报告编制基础的可接受性时,审计人员应当考虑企业的性质、财务报表的目的、财务报表的性质、法律法规是否规定了适用的财务报告编制基础。

【学习提示】

管理层和治理层有哪些责任?

管理层和治理层的责任包括:

1. 按照适用的财务报告编制基础编制财务报表,设计、执行和维护必要的内部控制,以使财务报表不存在由于舞弊或错误导致重大错报。

2. 向审计人员提供必要的工作条件,允许审计人员接触与编制财务报表相关的所有信息,以及提供审计所需要的其他信息,允许审计人员在获取审计证据时不受限制地接触其认为必要的内部人员和其他相关人员。

只有管理层、治理层愿意承担其对财务报表的责任,审计人员才能承担其对财务报表审计的责任。相反,如果管理层、治理层不认可他们的责任,审计人员执行审计工作的前提就不存在,此时审计人员就不能承接该财务报表审计。

The Audit Engagement Letter

The engagement letter is the written terms of an engagement in the form of a letter. It defines the legal relationship (or engagement) between a firm and its client(s). This letter states the terms and conditions of the engagement, principally addressing the scope of the engagement and the terms of compensation for the firm.

审计业务约定书

审计业务约定书是指会计师事务所与被审计单位签订的书面协议。它明确了会计师事务所和被审计单位之间的法律(或者业务)关系。这份约定书记录了业务的主要条款,包括业务的范围以及业务的收费等事项。会计师事务所承接任何审计业务,都应与被审计单位签订审计业务约定书。

Quality Control for an Audit of Financial Statements

The objective of the firm is to establish and maintain a system of quality control to provide it with reasonable assurance that: (a) The firm and its personnel comply with professional standards and applicable legal and regulatory requirements; and (b) Reports issued by the firm or engagement partners are appropriate in the circumstances.

The firm shall establish and maintain a system of quality control that includes policies and procedures that address each of the following elements: (a) Leadership responsibilities for quality within the firm; (b) Relevant ethical requirements; (c) Acceptance and continuance of client relationships and specific engagements; (d) Human resources; (e) Engagement performance; (f) Monitoring.

审计业务的质量控制

会计师事务所应当建立和维护质量控制制度,以合理保证:(1) 会计师事务所及其人员遵守法律法规和各项专业标准;(2) 会计师事务所和项目合伙人根据具体情况出具恰当的报告。

会计师事务所建立并维护的质量控制制度应当包括针对下列

要素而制定的政策和程序：(1) 公司内部对业务质量承担的领导责任；(2) 相关职业道德规范；(3) 客户关系和具体业务的接受与保持；(4) 人力资源；(5) 业务执行；(6) 监控。

【学习提示】

审计准则与审计质量控制的关系是什么？

如果说审计准则是审计人员的工作规则，那么审计业务的质量控制就是会计师事务所为了确保审计人员在处理每一项审计业务时都能够遵照审计准则的要求而制定和实施的一系列政策和程序。

A-5 Internal Audit / 内部审计

Internal Audit

Internal auditing is an appraisal or monitoring activity established or within an entity as a service to the entity. It functions by, among other things, examining, evaluating and reporting to management and the directors on the adequacy and effectiveness of internal control systems.

内部审计

内部审计，是建立于企业内部、服务于企业本身的一种评价和监督活动。它的主要职责是对会计和内部控制制度的充分性和有效性进行检查和评价，并且向管理层和董事会进行报告。

Value for Money Audits

Value for money（VFM）audits are audits of a not-for-profit organization（government agency or unit，charity，trust，etc.）to assess the economy，efficiency and effectiveness of activities and process. These are known as three Es VFM audits.

Economy：Attaining the appropriate quantity and quality of physical，human and financial resources（inputs）at lowest cost.

Efficiency：This is the relationship between goods or services produced（outputs）and the resources used to produce them.

Effectiveness：This is concerned with how well an activity is achieving its policy objectives or other intended effects.

效益审计

效益审计是指就非营利机构(包括政府部门、慈善机构、信托等)的各种活动的经济性、效益性和效果性做出综合性评价。效益审计也称 3E 审计。

经济是指用最少的耗费获得适当数量和质量的物质、人力和资金。它主要关注被审计单位各种资源耗费的节约，比如，原材料购置成本的节约、人工雇佣成本的节约等。审计人员需要评价被审计单位对各项经济资源的利用是否节约合理，并找出不节约、不合理的原因。

效率性是指投入资源和产出产品、服务或其他成果之间的关系，比如耗费同样的原材料生产出更多合格的产品，审计人员需要评价被审计单位的各项活动效率性目标的实现情况，如生产能力是否得到充分使用。

效果性，主要关注一项活动是否达到了其政策目标或其他期望的效果。它主要考查目标实现的程度，以及从事一项活动时期望取得的成果与实际取得的成果之间的关系。审计人员通过比较各项计划和目标的执行结果，并与预期结果进行比较，分析其出现差异的原因，为以后编制计划和制定目标提供资料和依据。

Outsourcing

Outsourcing is the use of external suppliers as a source of finished products, components or services. It is also known as sub-contracting.

外包

外包是指利用外部供应商提供产成品、部件或者服务，也称为分包。比如，企业可以将生产或经营过程中的某一个或某几个环节交给其他（专门）公司完成，或者将客户关系管理、仓储运输物流管理等服务活动外包。

【学习提示】

什么是内部审计外包？

内部审计外包是指由外部的服务机构，比如会计师事务所，为企业提供内部审计服务。在这种情况下，提供内部审计服务的人员不再是企业的员工，从而在一定程度上可以提高内部审计的独立性；同时，内部审计外包可以减少企业有关的管理成本，企业可以得到更专业、更灵活的内部审计服务。但是，内部审计外包也可能带来一些问题，比如，企业机密信息的泄露，审计人员的流动性大且缺乏对企业文化的深入了解。是否需要外包内部审计，企业应当充分考虑有关的成本和效益。

Part B

Planning and Risk Assessment / 审计计划和风险评估

B－1 Assessing Audit Risk / 评估审计风险

Risk Assessment Procedures

Risk assessment procedures are the audit procedures performed to obtain an understanding of the entity and its environment, including the entity's internal control, to identify and assess the risks of material misstatement, whether due to fraud or error, at the financial statement and assertion levels.

The risk assessment procedures shall include the following:

(a) Inquiries of management, of appropriate individuals within the internal audit function (if the function exists), and of others within the entity who in the auditor's judgment may have information that is likely to assist in identifying risks of material misstatement due to fraud or error.

(b) Analytical procedures.

(c) Observation and inspection.

风险评估程序

风险评估程序就是审计人员执行的，用以了解被审计单位及其环境，包括了解被审计单位的内部控制的程序。旨在识别和评估财务报表层次和认定层次存在重大错报的可能性，无论错报是舞弊导致的还是错误导致的。

风险评估程序包括：

1. 询问管理层和被审计单位内部其他人员，包括内部审计人员（如果被审计单位有内部审计职责）以及审计人员认为可能具备有助于识别重大错报风险的信息的其他人员。

2. 分析性程序。

3. 观察和检查。

【学习提示】

审计人员风险评估工作的实质是什么？

审计人员实施风险评估程序的目的在于了解被审计单位及其环境并评估财务报表层次和认定层次的重大错报风险。

一定要注意的是，在进行风险评估时，审计人员关注的是被审计单位财务报表的重大错报风险，而不是企业的经营风险。在风险评估阶段，审计人员了解企业的经营情况，最终目的是要把这些情况与财务报表的重大错报联系起来。所谓的风险应对，也就是针对审计人员识别的重大错报风险，设计审计程序。

比如，被审计单位销售毛利率过高，那么财务报表中销售收入截止这个认定可能存在重大错报，也就是说，被审计单位可能把下一个年度的销售收入提前确认了。那么相关的风险应对就是扩大销售收入的截止测试，尤其关注报表日前确认的销售交易，追查相关的出库单和发票，确保其出库日期确实是在报表日前。

Professional Skepticism

It is an attitude that includes a questing mind, being alert to conditions which may indicate possible misstatement due to error or fraud, and a critical assessment of audit evidence.

职业怀疑

职业怀疑是指审计人员执行审计业务的一种态度，包括采取质疑的思维方式，对可能表明由于错误或舞弊导致错报的迹象保持警觉，以及对审计证据进行审慎评价。

职业怀疑意味着，在进行询问和实施其他审计程序时，审计人员不能因轻信管理层和治理层的诚信而满足于说服力不够的审计证据。为得出审计结论，审计人员也不应当使用管理层声明替代应当获取的充分、适当的审计证据。

Audit Risk

Audit risk is the risk that the auditor expresses an inappropriate audit opinion when the financial statements are materially misstated. Audit risk is unavoidable because auditors gather evidence only on a test basis and because well-concealed frauds are extremely difficult to detect. Audit risk has two components, one is the risk of material misstatement, the other is the risk of detection.

审计风险

审计风险是指财务报表存在重大错报时，审计人员发表不恰当审计意见的可能性。审计风险是不可避免的，因为审计人员只是在测试的基础上收集审计证据，另外比较隐蔽的舞弊也是难以发现的。审计风险由两部分组成：一是重大错报风险，二是检查风险。

Business Risk

Business risk is a risk resulting from significant conditions, events, circumstances, actions or inactions that could adversely affect an entity's ability to achieve its objectives and execute its strategies, or from the setting of inappropriate objectives and strategies.

经营风险

经营风险源于对被审计单位实现目标和战略产生不利影响的重大情况、事项、环境和行动，或源于制定了不恰当的目标和战略。

具体而言，经营风险主要是指公司的决策人员和管理人员在经营管理中出现失误而导致公司盈利水平变化，从而产生投资者预期收益下降的风险，或由于汇率的变动而导致未来收益下降和成本增加。

Acceptable Audit Risk

Acceptable audit risk is a measure of how willing the auditor is to accept that the financial statements may be materially misstated after the audit is completed and an unqualified opinion has been issued.

可接受审计风险

可接受审计风险是指审计人员在完成审计工作以后愿意承担

的、对存在重大错报的财务报表出具无保留审计意见的风险。

在确定可接受的审计风险时，需要考虑审计人员对审计风险的态度、审计失败对审计人员可能造成的损失大小等因素。由于审计业务是一种保证程度较高的鉴证业务，可接受的审计风险应当足够低。可接受的审计风险越低，意味着审计人员需要收集的审计证据越多。

Risk of Material Misstatement

Risk of material misstatement is the risk that the financial statements are materially misstated. It is dependent on the entity. It has two components — inherent risk and control risk.

重大错报风险

重大错报风险就是企业财务报表存在重大错报的可能性。它取决于被审计单位。它有两个组成部分——固有风险和控制风险。

重大错报风险与被审计单位的经营风险相关，且独立存在于财务报表审计中。这是审计人员无法控制的风险。

【学习提示】

如何区分经营风险与审计风险？

在分析审计风险时，我们常常把经营风险和审计风险混为一谈。经营风险是企业本身的风险，而审计风险则是审计人员未能发现重大错报而给出不适当的审计报告的风险。在分析审计风险时，我们关注的是财务报表的认定出现错报的可能性。比如，当我们发现被审计单位的存货周转率下降时，对于企业而言，其经营风险就是存货滞销或者积压占用过多的流动资金；而站在审计人员的角度，我们关注的是被审计单位存货可变现净值可能会低于其成本。如果被审计单位没有增加计提存货减值准备，则资产负债表里的存货就可能被高估，也就是存货的计价可能存在重大错报风险。

Inherent Risk

Inherent risk is the susceptibility of an assertion to a misstatement that could be material, either individually or when aggregated with other misstatements, assuming there were no related internal controls.

Inherent risk is affected by the nature of an entity and factors which can result in an increase include:

- Changes in the industry it operates in;
- Operations that are subject to a high degree of regulation;
- Going concern and liquidity issues including loss of significant customers;
- Developing or offering new products or services, or moving into new lines of business;
- Expanding into new locations;
- Application of new accounting standards;
- Accounting measurements that involve complex processes;
- Events or transactions that involve significant accounting estimates;
- Pending litigation and contingent liabilities.

固有风险

固有风险是指在考虑相关的内部控制之前，某一认定易于发生错报(该错报单独或连同其他错报可能是重大的)的可能性。

固有风险主要受被审计单位性质所影响,下列因素或导致固有风险增加:

- 所处行业发生变化;
- 经营活动受高度管制;
- 持续经营或流动性出现问题,比如失去重要的客户;
- 开发新产品或提供新服务或者进入新的业务线;
- 扩张至新的地域;
- 采用新会计准则;
- 会计计量过程复杂;
- 涉及重大会计估计的交易或事项;
- 未决诉讼和或有负债。

Control Risk

Control risk is the risk that a misstatement, that could occur in an assertion and that could be material, either individually or when aggregated with other misstatements, will not be prevented or detected and corrected on a timely basis by the entity's internal control.

The following factors can result in an increase in control risk:

- Lack of personnel with appropriate accounting and financial reporting skills;
- Changes in key personnel including departure of key management;
- Deficiencies in internal control, especially those not addressed by management;

- Changes in the information technology (IT) environment;
- Installation of significant new IT systems related to financial reporting.

控制风险

控制风险是指某一认定发生错报，该错报单独或连同其他错报可能是重大的，但没有被内部控制及时防止或发现并纠正的可能性。

控制风险取决于与财务报表编制有关的内部控制的设计和运行的有效性。由于内部控制的固有局限性，某种程度的控制风险始终存在。

下列因素会导致控制风险的增加：

- 会计和财务报告技能的人员缺乏；
- 关键人员变更，包括关键管理人员的离职；
- 内部控制的缺陷，尤其是那些管理层没有提及的漏洞；
- 信息技术环境的变化；
- 安装新的与财务报告相关的重要的信息系统。

Detection Risk

Detection risk is the risk that the procedures performed by the auditor to reduce audit risk to an acceptably low level will not detect a misstatement that exists and that could be material, either individually or when aggregated with other misstatements.

检查风险

检查风险是指如果存在某一错报，该错报单独或连同其他错报可能是重大的，审计人员将审计风险降至可接受的低水平而实施程序后没有发现这种错报的风险。

检查风险取决于审计程序设计的合理性和执行的有效性。

由于审计人员通常并不对所有的交易、账户余额和披露进行检查，以及其他原因，检查风险不可能降低为零。其他原因包括审计人员可能选择了不恰当的审计程序、审计过程执行不当，或者错误地解读了审计结论。

【学习提示】

固有风险、控制风险、重大错报风险、检查风险以及审计风险之间的关系是什么？

固有风险是指不考虑内部控制，某项目本身出错的可能性，比如现金的流动性高于固定资产，更容易被偷盗，因此现金的固有风险高于固定资产。控制风险是指当错报发生了，企业内部控制系统未能及时防止、发现和更正。比如，当我们在进行会计处理时，出现了一项重大错报，这就是固有风险；而相关的内部审核人员并没有发现这项错报，内控失效，这就是控制风险。于是财务报表就出现了重大错报，这就是重大错报风险。（因此，我们说重大错报风险是由固有风险和控制风险构成的。）如果审计人员在审计过程中也没有发现这项错报，这就是检查风险。最终，审计人员给出了不恰当的审计意见，这就是审计风险。

Materiality

Misstatements, including omissions, are considered to be material if they, either individually or in the aggregate, could reasonably be expected to influence the economic decisions of users taken on the basis of the financial statements.

重要性

如果一项错报，包括漏报，单独或连同其他错报可能影响财务报表使用者依据财务报表做出的经济决策，则该项错报是重大的。

重要性取决于在具体环境下对错报金额和性质的判断。

Performance Materiality

Performance materiality is the amount or amounts set by the auditor at less than materiality for the financial statements as a whole to reduce an appropriately low level the probability that the aggregate of uncorrected and undetected misstatements exceeds materiality for the financial statements as a whole. It also refers to the amounts set by the auditor at less than the materiality level of levels for particular classes of transactions, account balances or disclosures.

实际执行的重要性

实际执行的重要性是指审计人员确定的低于财务报表整体的重要性的一个或多个金额，旨在将未更正和未发现错报的汇总数超过财务报表整体的重要性的可能性降至适当的低水平。它还指审计人员确定的低于特定类别的交易、账户余额或披露的重要性水平的一个或多个金额。

确定实际执行的重要性并非简单机械的计算，需要审计人员运用职业判断，并考虑下列因素：

1. 对被审计单位的了解（这些了解在实施风险评估程序的过程中得到更新）；

2. 前期审计工作中识别出的错报的性质和范围；

3. 根据前期识别出的错报对本期错报做出的预期。

通常而言,实际执行的重要性一般为财务报表整体重要性的50%～75%。

【学习提示】

如何正确理解重要性这个概念?

重要性概念可从以下三个方面理解:

1. 如果合理预期错报(包括漏报)单独或汇总起来可能影响财务报表使用者依据财务报表做出的经济决策,则通常认为错报是重大的。

2. 对重要性的判断是根据具体环境做出的,并受错报的金额或性质的影响,或受两者共同作用的影响。

3. 判断某事项对财务报表使用者是否重大,是在考虑财务报表使用者整体共同的财务信息需求的基础上做出的。

审计的重要性主要运用在两个环节:一是在计划和执行财务报表审计工作时,审计人员运用重要性对重大金额的错报做出判断;二是在确定审计意见类型时,审计人员需要考虑重要性水平,评价识别出的错报对审计的影响,以及评价未更正错报对财务报表的影响。

确定重要性水平是审计计划阶段的一项重要工作。它实质上是审计人员对错报的容忍程度。审计人员认为超过重要性水平的错报会影响投资者的决策,被审计单位必须调整这类错报,否则就不可以出具无保留意见的审计报告。对重要性的判断需要依赖审计人员的专业判断,并且随着审计工作的展开、审计人员对被审计单位的了解逐渐深入,重要性水平也需要持续修订。对重要性水平的修订贯穿整个审计工作过程。

Significant Risk

Significant risks are complex or unusual transactions that may indicate fraud, or other special risks. They are those that require special audit consideration.

In exercising judgment as to which risks are significant risks, the auditor shall consider at least the followings:

(a) Whether the risk is a risk of fraud;

(b) Whether the risk is related to recent significant economic, accounting or other developments and, therefore, requires specific attention;

(c) The complexity of transactions;

(d) Whether the risk involves significant transactions with related parties;

(e) The degree of subjectivity in the measurement of financial information related to the risk, especially those measurements involving a wide range of measurement uncertainty; and

(f) Whether the risk involves significant transactions that are outside the normal course of business for the entity, or that otherwise appear to be unusual.

特别风险

特别风险是指那些复杂的或非常规的、有舞弊迹象的交易，或者其他特别的风险。它们是需要审计人员异常关注的特别的重大错报风险。

在确定风险是否为特别风险时，审计人员至少应当考虑下列因素：

1. 风险是否属于舞弊风险；

2. 风险是否与近期经济环境、会计处理方法和其他方面的重大变化有关，从而需要特别注意；

3. 交易的复杂程度；

4. 风险是否涉及重大的关联方交易；

5. 财务信息计量的主观程度，特别是对不确定事项的计量存在较大区间；

6. 风险是否涉及异常或超出正常经营过程的重大交易。

Test of Control

Test of controls are audit procedures designed to evaluate the operating effectiveness of controls in preventing, or detecting and correcting, material misstatements at the assertion level.

In designing and performing tests of controls, the auditor shall obtain audit evidence about the operating effectiveness of the controls, including:

(a) How the controls were applied at relevant times during the period under audit;

(b) The consistency with which they were applied; and

(c) By whom or by what means they were applied.

控制测试

控制测试是指用于评价内部控制在防止或发现并纠正认定层次重大错报方面的运行有效性的审计程序。

在设计和执行控制测试时，审计人员应当就下列方面获取关于控制有效运行的审计证据：

1. 控制在所审计期间的相关时点是如何运行的；

2. 控制是否得到一贯执行；

3. 控制由谁或以何种方式执行。

Substantive Procedure

Substantive procedures are audit procedures designed to detect material misstatements at the assertion level. Substantive procedures comprise：

(a) Tests of details (of classes of transactions, account balances, and disclosures); and

(b) Substantive analytical procedures.

实质性程序

实质性程序是指用于发现认定层次重大错报的审计程序。实质性程序包括：

1. 对各类交易、账户余额和披露的细节测试；

2. 实质性分析程序。

【学习提示】

1. 如何区分细节测试与实质性分析程序？

实质性测试包括细节测试和实质性分析程序。细节测试是对各类交易、账户余额、列报的具体细节进行测试，目的在于直接识别财务报表认定是否存在错报。实质性分析程序从技术上讲仍然是分析程序，主要是通过研究数据间的关系来评价信息的合理性。只是将该技术方法用作实质性程序，即用以识别各类交易、账户余额、列报及相关认定是否可能存在错报，至于错报的金额是多少，则只能通过细节测试来确定。比如，审计人员通过分析审计年度的存货周转率，认为期末存货很可能存在重大错报，但并不能确定具体的错报金额是多少，这就是分析程序。接下来，审计人员可以通过对存货实施盘点程序（属于细节测试）并结合其他细节测试来确定存货的错报金额的具体数字。

2. 如何区分控制测试与实质性测试？如何设计有效的审计程序？

问题的关键是要明确执行审计程序的目的。控制测试的目的是为了验证内部控制运行的有效性，因此，设计控制测试程序的前提是了解被审计单位的相关内部控制系统，然后收集证据证明该制度、政策或者程序已经得到有效遵循。而实质性程序的目的直接与财务报表的认定相关联。设计出有效的实质性程序的关键是了解与被审计单位有关的会计信息系统及其流程（包括交易的发起、执行、记录和报告，以及重要的信息载体，比如关键的原始凭证、账簿记录），然后结合财务报表认定收集相关的证据。

3. 何时需要执行控制测试？

关于控制测试，一定要注意：审计人员在了解被审计单位的内部控制之后，预计相关的控制风险程度为中等或低，并且准备依赖相关的内部控制时，或者仅依靠实质性测试无法获得充分适当的审计证据时，审计人员才需要执行控制测试，以支持自己对控制风险的评价。如果被审计单位的内部控制很差，预计控制风险很高，则审计人员会放弃控制测试而直接进行实质性程序。

另外，控制测试的目的是减少实质性测试。通过控制测试，审计人员确信被审计单位的内部控制政策和程序都得到正确的执行时，才能减少实质性测试审计程序，从而减少审计取证工作，提高审计工作的效率。如果进行了控制测试却无法减少实质性测试，审计人员也会放弃控制测试，比如所有者权益的审计。由于所有者权益项目增减变动的次数比较少，而增减变动的金额都比较大，因此，审计人员往往会采用详细审计，这时控制测试的作用就不明显了。

Fraud

Fraud is an intentional act by one or more individuals among management, those charged with governance, employees or third parties involving the use of deception to obtain an unjust or illegal advantage.

舞弊

舞弊是指被审计单位的管理层、治理层、员工或第三方使用欺骗手段获取不当或非法利益的故意行为。

舞弊是一个宽泛的法律概念，但在财务报表审计中，审计人员关注的是导致财务报表重大错报的舞弊。

Fraudulent Financial Reporting

Fraudulent financial reporting involves intentional misstatement, including omissions of amounts or disclosures in financial, to deceive financial statement users.

编制虚假财务报告

编制虚假财务报告涉及为欺骗财务报表使用者而做出故意错报，包括故意漏报金额或财务报表披露。

编制虚假财务报告包括对编制财务报表所依据的会计记录或支持性文件进行操纵、弄虚作假（伪造）或篡改等行为；在财务报表中错误表达或故意漏记事项、交易或其他重要信息；以及故意地错误使用与金额、分类、列报或披露相关的会计原则。

Misappropriation of Assets

Misappropriation of assets involves the theft of an entity's assets and is often perpetrated by employees in relatively small and immaterial amounts. It can also involve management who are usually more capable of disguising or concealing misappropriations in ways that are difficult to detect.

侵占资产

侵占资产包括盗窃被审计单位的资产，通常的做法是员工盗窃金额相对较小且不重要的资产。侵占资产也可能涉及管理层，他们通常更能够通过难以发现的手段掩饰或隐瞒侵占资产的行为。

侵占资产可以通过以下方式实现：

1. 贪污收到的款项；

2. 盗窃实物资产或无形资产；

3. 使被审计单位为未收到的商品或未接受的劳务付款；

4. 将被审计单位资产挪为私用。

【学习提示】

审计人员对财务报表舞弊应该承担什么责任?

舞弊实质上是一个法律概念，但在财务报表审计中，审计人员关注的首先是导致财务报表发生重大错报的舞弊。我们应该认识到，被审计单位的治理层和管理层对防止或发现舞弊负有主要责任。审计人员对发现舞弊的责任可以从以下两个方面进行界定：

1. 在按照审计准则的规定执行审计工作时，审计人员有责任对财务报表整体是否不存在由于舞弊或错误导致的重大错报获取合理保证。

2. 由于审计的固有限制，即使审计人员按照审计准则的规定恰当计划和执行了审计工作，也不可避免地存在财务报表中的某些重大错报未被发现的风险。

因此，如果在审计工作中审计人员未能识别出舞弊导致的财务报表重大错报，并不必然表示审计人员没有遵守审计准则。

B－2 Audit Planning and Documentation / 审计计划和审计工作底稿

Overall Audit Strategy

The overall audit strategy sets the scope, timing and direction of the audit, and guides the development of the more detailed audit plan. The overall audit strategy includes the followings:

(a) **Characteristics of the Engagement:** the financial reporting framework, industry-specific reporting requirements and the expected audit coverage, etc.

(b) **Reporting Objectives, Timing of the Audit, and Nature of Communications:** the entity's timetable for reporting, the organization of meetings with management and those charged with governance to discuss the nature, timing and extent of the audit work, etc.

(c) **Significant Factors, Preliminary Engagement Activities, and Knowledge Gained on Other Engagements:** the determination of materiality, the preliminary identification of significant components and material classes of transactions, account balances and disclosures, preliminary identification of areas where there may be a higher risk of material misstatement, etc.

(d) **Nature, Timing and Extent of Resources:** the selection of the engagement team and the assignment of audit work to the team members, including the assignment of appropriately experienced team members to areas where there may be higher risks of material misstatement.

总体审计策略

总体审计策略用以确定审计范围、时间和方向，并指导制定具体审计计划。总体审计计划主要包括四个部分的内容：

1. 业务的特征，包括拟审计财务信息所依据的财务报告编制基础、特定行业的报告要求，以及预期审计工作涵盖的范围(其中包括应涵盖的组成部分的数量及所在地点)，等等。

2. 报告目标、时间安排及所需要沟通的性质，包括被审计单位对外报告的时间表；与管理层和治理层举行会谈，讨论审计工作的性质和时间安排及范围等。

3. 重大事项、初步业务活动以及其他业务所获得的信息，包括确定重要性水平；初步识别重要的组成部分，重大类别的交易、账户余额和披露；初步识别可能存在较高的重大错报风险领域；等等。

4. 审计资源的性质、时间和范围，包括调配项目小组以及将重大错报风险较高的领域分派给经验丰富的小组成员等。

Audit Plan

The audit plan converts the audit strategy into a more

detailed plan and includs the nature, timing, and extent of audit procedures to be performed by engagement team members in order to obtain sufficient appropriate audit evidence to reduce audit risk to an acceptably low level.

具体审计计划

具体审计计划是依据总体审计策略制定的更详细的计划,包括为收集充分、适当的审计证据而将审计风险降低至可接受的低水平,以及项目组成员拟实施的审计程序的性质、时间和范围。

【学习提示】

总体审计策略与具体审计计划有何差异?

审计计划分为总体审计策略和具体审计计划两个层次。审计人员首先根据对被审计单位经营环境的了解,评估重大错报风险,然后制定总体审计策略。其次,审计人员应当针对总体审计策略中所识别的不同事项,制定具体审计计划。总体审计策略针对整个审计业务而言,是制定具体审计计划的指南。而具体审计计划则是针对每一项重要的账户余额或交易。完整详细的进一步审计程序的计划包括对各类交易、账户余额和披露实施的具体审计程序的性质、时间和范围,包括抽取的样本量等。

Audit Documentation

Audit documentation is the record of audit procedures performed, relevant audit evidence obtained and conclusions reached.

审计工作底稿

审计工作底稿，是指审计人员对实施的审计程序、获取的相关审计证据，以及得出的审计结论做出的记录。

审计工作底稿是审计人员在审计工作过程中形成的全部审计工作记录和获取的资料。它是审计证据的载体，可作为审计过程和结果的书面证明，也是形成审计结论的依据。

【学习提示】

在计划阶段如何进行风险评估和风险应对？

在审计的计划阶段，审计人员首先要通过了解被审计单位的基本情况，通过执行风险评估程序来识别被审计单位财务报表可能出现的重大错报风险。有些风险可能导致整个财务报表的多个项目出现重大错报，比如管理层面临异常的压力，这就是财务报表层次的重大错报风险。更多的风险则与财务报表的认定相关。

我们评估风险的最主要的目的就是把风险与财务报表相关认定的错报相联系，才能设计适当的审计程序应对识别的审计风险。比如，我们发现被审计单位的销售毛利率远远超过行业平均水平，这时我们就有理由相信财务报表中的销售收入的截止这项认定可能存在错报，也就是说，被审计单位可能将下期的销售提前确认。因此，在进一步的审计程序中，我们就需要扩大销售收入截止测试的范围，而且重点关注发货日期是否在资产负债表日前，有无将资产负债表日以后的发货确认为当期的销售收入。

Part C

Internal Control / 内部控制

C-1 Internal Control Systems / 内部控制系统

Internal Control

Internal control is the process designed, implemented and maintained by those charged with governance, management, and other personnel to provide reasonable assurance about the achievement of the entity's objectives with regard to reliability of financial reporting, effectiveness and efficiency of operations, and compliance with applicable laws and regulations. Internal control has five components: the control environment, the entity's risk assessment process, the information system relevant to financial reporting, control activities, monitoring of controls.

内部控制

内部控制是单位为了合理保证财务报告的可靠性、经营的效率和效果以及对法律法规的遵守，由治理层、管理层和其他人员设计与执行的政策与程序。内部控制包括五个要素：控制环境、风险评估过程、与财务报告相关的信息系统和沟通、控制活动、对控制的监督。

Control Environment

Control environment includes the governance and management functions and the attitudes, awareness and actions of those charged with governance and management concerning the entity's internal control and its importance in the entity.

The control environment encompasses the following elements:

(a) Communication and enforcement of integrity and ethical values.

(b) Commitment to competence.

(c) Participation by those charged with governance.

(d) Management's philosophy and operating style.

(e) Organizational structure.

(f) Assignment of authority and responsibility.

(g) Human resource policies and practices.

控制环境

控制环境包括治理职能和管理职能，以及治理层和管理层对内部控制及其重要性的态度、认识和措施。

控制环境设定了该单位的内部控制的基调，影响员工对内部控制的意识。良好的控制环境是实施有效内部控制的基础。

控制环境包括：

1. 对诚信和道德价值观念的沟通与落实。对诚信和道德价值观念的沟通与落实，既包括管理层如何处理不诚实、非法或不道德的行为，也包括在被审计单位内部，通过行为规范以及高层管理人员的身体力行，对诚实和道德价值观念的营造和保持。

2. 对胜任能力的重视。管理层对胜任能力的重视包括对于特定工作所需的胜任能力水平的设定，以及对达到该水平所必需的知识和能力的要求。

3. 治理层的参与程度。治理层对控制环境的影响因素主要包括：治理层相对于管理层的独立性、成员的经验和品德、治理层参与被审计单位经营的程度和收到的信息及其对经营活动的详细检查、治理层采取措施的适当性等。

4. 管理层的理念和经营风格。管理层的理念包括管理层对内部控制的理念，即管理层对内部控制以及具体实施环境的重视程度。管理层的经营风格可以表明管理层所能接受的业务风险的性质。

5. 组织结构。被审计单位的组织结构为计划、运作、控制及监督经营活动提供了一个整体框架。

6. 职权与责任的分配。通过集权或分权决策，可在不同部门间进行适当的职责划分，建立适当层次的报告体系。组织结构将影响权力、责任和工作任务在组织成员中的分配。

7. 人力资源政策与实务。人力资源政策与实务涉及招聘、培训、考核、咨询、晋升和薪酬等方面。

The Entity's Risk Assessment Process

For financial reporting purposes, the entity's risk assessment process includes how management identifies business risks relevant to the preparation of financial statements in accordance with the entity's applicable financial reporting framework, estimates their significance, assesses the likelihood of their occurrence, and decides upon actions to respond to and manage them and the results thereof.

风险评估过程

为财务报告的目的，被审计单位风险评估过程包括：管理层如何识别与财务报表相关的经营风险；如何估计该风险的重要性；如何评估风险发生的可能性；如何采取措施管理这些风险。

The Information System Relevant to Financial Reporting

The information system relevant to financial reporting is a component of internal control that includes the financial reporting system, and consists of the procedures and records established to initiate, record, process and report entity transactions (as well as events and conditions) and to maintain accountability for the related assets, liabilities and equity.

The information system relevant to financial reporting objectives, which includes the financial reporting system, encompasses methods and records that:

(a) Identify and record all valid transactions;

(b) Describe on a timely basis the transactions in sufficient detail to permit proper classification of transactions for financial reporting;

(c) Measure the value of transactions in a manner that permits recording their proper monetary value in the financial statements;

(d) Determine the time period in which transactions occurred to permit recording of transactions in the proper accounting period;

(e) Present properly the transactions and related disclosures in the financial statements.

与财务报告相关的信息系统

与财务报告相关的信息系统是内部控制的组成部分，包括用以生成、记录、处理和报告交易、事项和情况，对相关资产、负债和所有者权益履行经营管理责任的程序和记录。

与财务报告相关的信息系统包括下列职能：

1. 识别与记录所有的有效交易；

2. 及时、详细地描述交易，以便在财务报告中对交易做出恰当分类；

3. 确定交易的金额，以便在财务报表中对交易的金额做出准确记录；

4. 确定交易发生的时间，以便将交易记录在正确的会计期间；

5. 在财务报表中恰当地列报交易以及相关信息的披露。

Control Activities

Control activities are those policies and procedures that help ensure that management directive are carried out. Examples of specific control activities include those relation to：

Authorisation — approval of transactions by a suitably responsible official to ensure transactions are genuine.

Performance Reviews — comparison or review of the performance of the business to identify unusual differences between data.

Information Processing — computer controls including general IT controls, which cover a range of applications and support the overall IT environment and application controls which are manual or automated controls which operate on a cycle/business process level.

Physical Controls — restricting access to physical assets such as cash, inventory and plant and equipment, thereby reducing the risk of theft, and the authorization for access to computer programs and data files, the periodic counting and comparison with amounts shown on control records.

Segregation of Duties — assignment of roles/responsibilities to different people, thereby reducing the risk of fraud and error occurring.

控制活动

控制活动是指有助于确保管理层的指令得以执行的政策和程序。具体包括与授权、业绩评价、信息处理、实物控制和职责分离等相关的活动。

授权：业务在执行之前应当经过相关责任人的授权，以保证交易的真实性。

业绩评价：通过比较和评价业务的执行情况，以发现数据中的异常差异。比如评价实际业绩与预算、预测或前期业绩，以发现异常差异并采取必要的调查和纠正措施。

信息处理：计算机内部控制主要包括信息技术的一般控制和应用控制。一般控制涵盖多个应用系统并且支持整个IT环境，应用控制是指在业务流程或循环层面的人工或自动化的控制。

实物控制：主要包括限制接近某些有形资产，如现金、存货或固定资产等，以减少被偷盗的风险；另外，对访问计算机程序和数据文件设置授权，以及定期盘点，并将盘点记录与会计记录核对。

职责分离：将不同的职责分配给不同的员工，以降低舞弊的风险和错误的发生。一般而言,交易的授权、交易的记录以及保管资产的职责应当由不同的员工履行。

Monitoring Control

Monitoring control is a process to assess the effectiveness of internal control performance over time. It includes assessing the design and operation of controls on a timely basis and taking necessary corrective actions modified for changes in conditions. Monitoring of controls may include activities such as management's review of whether bank reconciliations are being prepared on a timely basis, internal auditors' evaluation of sales personnel's compliance with the entity's policies on terms of sales contracts, and a legal department's oversight of compliance with the entity's ethical or business practice policies. Monitoring is done also to ensure that controls continue to operate effectively over time. For example, if the timeliness and accuracy of bank reconciliations are not monitored, personnel are likely to stop preparing them.

对控制的监督

对控制的监督是指被审计单位评价内部控制在一段时间运行有效性的过程。对控制的监督涉及及时评估控制的有效性并采取必要的补救措施。对控制的监督主要包括:管理层对是否及时编制银行存款余额调节表进行复核;内部审计人员评价销售人员是否遵守公司关于销售合同条款的政策;法律部门定期监控公司的道德规范和商务行为准则是否都已遵循等。监督也是为了确保控制能够持续有效地运行。例如,如果没有对银行存款余额调节表是否得到及时和准确地编制进行监督，那么员工就很可能停止编制该表。

C－2 The Use and Evaluation of Internal Control Systems by Auditors / 审计人员对内部控制系统的使用和评价

Documenting the Client Systems

Auditors commonly use four types of documents to document their understanding of the design of internal control: narrative notes, flowcharts, internal control questionnaires and internal control evaluation questionnaires.

Narrative Notes — a written description of a client's internal control.

Flowchart — a diagram of the client's documents and their sequential flow in the organization.

Internal Control Questionnaire (ICQ) — a list of controls given to the client to say whether or not those controls are in place.

Internal Control Evaluation Questionnaire (ICE) — the client is asked what controls they have in place for a given control objective.

记录对内部控制的了解

审计人员通常会用四种方法记录他们对客户内部控制的了解：文字说明法、流程图法、内部控制问卷和内部控制评估问卷。

文字说明法：对被审计单位内部控制的书面说明。审计人员将被审计单位内部控制的调查结果，以简洁的文字加以叙述。其优点是可以对调查对象做出比较深入和具体的描述，而且使用范围广泛，不受企业类型的限制。但是有时候审计人员难以用简明的语言描述内部控制系统的细节。对于那些规模较大、内部控制较为复杂的企业，用文字说明势必显得冗长、头绪繁多，不便从总体上对内部控制系统做出全面评价。

流程图法：用图解的形式来描述被审计单位的记录以及它们在整个组织中的流动顺序。审计人员用特定的符号和图形来描述某项业务的整个处理过程，将凭证和记录的产生、传递、检查、保存及其相互关系，用图解的形式直观地表达出来。运用流程图可以将各项业务活动的职责分工、授权批准和复核验证等项控制措施与功能完整地显示出来，并且形象直观，能够突出现有的控制点，有助于审计人员全面了解内部控制系统的运行情况，及时识别系统中的不足之处，也便于审计人员随时根据业务控制程序的变化对流程图做出修改。但是由于缺少文字说明，较复杂的业务不易被人理解，而且绘制流程图需要一定的技术，尤其是较复杂的业务，绘制难度更大。

内部控制问卷：在该环节，审计人员将提出关键内控程序或政策的问题，客户只需要回答这些内部控制政策或程序是否存在。

内部控制评估问卷：在该环节，审计人员将询问客户用了哪些控制方法来达到既定的控制目标。

内部控制问卷和内部控制评估问卷都是调查表法。调查表的编制比较简单，但是由于调查表缺乏弹性，难以适用于各类型企业，尤其是小型企业或特殊行业的企业，往往会因不适用的回答太多而影响调查效果。

Walk-through Test

In order to confirm their understanding of the control system, auditor will pick up a transaction and follow it through the system to see whether all the controls they anticipate should be in existence were in operation with regard to that transaction.

穿行测试

穿行测试是指审计人员为了确认他们对被审计单位内部控制系统的了解,往往会选取一笔交易,并且追踪这些交易在财务报告信息系统中的处理过程,以确定所有相关控制是否与之前了解的情况相符,以及该项控制是否得到执行。

【学习提示】

穿行测试是控制测试吗?

穿行测试与控制测试的目的完全不同。控制测试的目的是验证内部控制的有效性,但穿行测试的目的仅仅是了解和评估内部控制。从选样的要求来看,执行穿行测试往往只需要抽取一笔或者几笔交易就可以,而控制测试的范围则取决于审计人员的职业判断,样本规模受交易发生的频率、拟信赖的控制时间长度、预期偏差、其他审计证据、审计证据的可靠性和相关性等因素的影响。

Deficiency in Internal Control

A deficiency in internal control exists when:

(a) A control is designed, implemented or operated in such a way that it is unable to prevent, or detect and correct, misstatements in the financial statements on a timely basis; or

(b) A control necessary to prevent, or detect and correct, misstatements in the financial statements on a timely basis is missing.

A significant deficiency in internal control is a deficiency or combination of deficiencies in internal control that, in the auditor's professional judgment, is of sufficient importance to merit the attention of those charged with governance.

Examples of matters that the auditor may consider in determining whether a deficiency or combination of deficiencies in internal control constitutes a significant deficiency include:

(a) The likelihood of the deficiencies leading to material misstatements in the financial statements in the future.

(b) The susceptibility to loss or fraud of the related asset or liability.

(c) The subjectivity and complexity of determining estimated amounts, such as fair value accounting estimates.

内部控制的缺陷

内部控制的缺陷是指一项控制的设计、执行或运行的方式不能够及时地防止、发现和更正财务报表的错报;或者缺乏某项能够及时防止、发现和更正财务报表错报的必要的控制。

内部控制的重大缺陷是指,根据审计人员的职业判断,内部控制中一项或多项缺陷非常重大,足以引起治理层的关注。

在确定内部控制中的一项或多项缺陷是否重大时,审计人员主要考虑:

1. 该项缺陷导致财务报表将来出现重大错报的可能性。

2. 相关资产和负债出现损失或舞弊的可能性。

3. 在确定估计金额时的主观性和复杂程度，如公允价值的会计估计。

【学习提示】

外部审计人员为什么需要了解被审计单位的内部控制？

审计人员在风险评估中了解内部控制的目的是评估财务报表出现重大错报的可能性。审计人员首先应该通过询问被审计单位管理人员，查阅以前年度工作底稿或者阅读有关内部控制生成的文件和记录等了解被审计单位的相关内部控制。然后用适当的方式把他们对内部控制的了解记录下来。为了确认所记录的内容的正确性，审计人员可以进行穿行测试。最后，审计人员应根据对内部控制的了解，评价内部控制的缺陷，将内部控制的缺陷与财务报表错报相关联，以此估计可能存在的重大错报风险。

Internal Controls in a Computerised Environment

The internal controls in a computerised environment include manual procedures and procedures designed into computer programs. Such controls are normally divided into two categories: general controls and application controls.

IT General Controls

IT general controls are policies and procedures that relate to many applications. They support the effective functioning of application controls by helping to ensure the continued proper operation of information systems. They include controls over the information technology (IT) environment, computer operations, access to programs and data, program development and program changes.

IT Application Controls

IT application controls are either manual or automated procedures and typically operate at the business process level. Application controls relate to data integrity and ensure that only valid data is being processed and is being processed completely and accurately.

信息技术环境下的内部控制

在信息技术环境下，内部控制既有传统的人工控制，也包括由计算机程序执行的控制。这些控制通常被划分为两类：一般控制和应用控制。

信息技术一般控制

信息技术一般控制是指与多个应用系统有关的政策和程序，有助于保证信息系统持续恰当地运行，支持应用控制作用的有效发挥。信息技术一般控制包括对信息技术环境、计算机运行、程序和数据访问、程序开发和程序变更等方面的控制。

信息技术应用控制

信息技术应用控制既可能是人工控制也可能是自动化控制，它们是在业务流程层面运行的控制。应用控制主要关注数据的完整性和准确性，确保完整、正确地处理真实有效的数据。应用控制与用于生成、记录、处理、报告交易或其他财务数据程序相关，一般经过输入、处理及输出等环节。

信息技术一般控制是控制的基础，信息技术一般控制的有效与否直接关系到信息技术应用控制的有效性是否能够信任。

Part D

Audit Evidence / 审计证据

D－1 Financial Statement Assertions / 财务报表的认定

Financial Statement Assertions

Financial statement assertions are the representations by management, explicit or otherwise, that are embodied in the financial statements, as used by the auditor to consider the different types of potential misstatements that may occur.

Assertions used by the auditor in considering the different types of potential misstatements that may occur may fall into the following categories: (a) assertions about classes of transactions and events, and related disclosures, for the period under audit; (b) assertions about account balances, and related disclosures, at the period end.

财务报表的认定

财务报表的认定是指管理层在财务报表中做出的明确或隐含的表达，审计人员将其用于考虑可能发生的不同类型的潜在错报。

认定与审计目标密切相关，审计人员的基本职责就是确定被审计单位管理层对其财务报表的认定是否恰当。

审计人员主要使用下列两类财务报表的认定来考虑可能发生的不同类型的潜在错报：(1) 关于审计期间各类交易和事项以及相关披露的认定；(2) 关于期末账户余额以及相关披露的认定。

Assertions About Classes of Transactions and Events, and Related Disclosures, for the Period Under Audit:

Occurrence — transactions and events that have been recorded or disclosed, have occurred, and such transactions and events pertain to the entity.

Completeness — all transactions and events that should have been recorded have been recorded, and all related disclosures that should have been included in the financial statements have been included.

Accuracy — amounts and other data relating to recorded transactions and events have been recorded appropriately, and related disclosures have been appropriately measured and described.

Cutoff — transactions and events have been recorded in the correct accounting period.

Classification — transactions and events have been recorded in the proper accounts.

Presentation — transactions and events are appropriately aggregated or disaggregated and clearly described, and related disclosures are relevant and understandable in the context of the requirements of the applicable financial reporting framework.

关于审计期间各类交易和事项以及相关披露的认定

发生：所记录和披露的交易和事项已发生且与被审计单位有关。

完整性：所有应当记录的交易和事项均已记录，并且所有与之相关应当包括在财务报表中的披露均已包括。

准确性：与交易和事项有关的金额及其他数据已恰当记录，与之相关的披露已恰当计量和描述。

截止：交易和事项已记录于正确的会计期间。

分类：交易和事项已记录于恰当的账户。

列报：交易和事项已经恰当地汇总或分解，并且清楚地表述，根据适用的财务报告框架，与之相关的披露是相关的和可理解的。

Assertions About Account Balances, and Related Disclosures, at the Period End:

Existence — assets, liabilities, and equity interests exist.

Rights and Obligations — the entity holds or controls the rights to assets, and liabilities are the obligations of the entity.

Completeness — all assets, liabilities and equity interests that should have been recorded have been recorded, and all related disclosures that should have been included in the financial statements have been included.

Accuracy, Valuation and Allocation — assets, liabilities, and equity interests have been included in the financial statements at appropriate amounts and any resulting valuation or allocation adjustments have been appropriately recorded, and related disclosures have been appropriately measured and described.

Classification — assets, liabilities and equity interests have been recorded in the proper accounts.

Presentation — assets, liabilities and equity interests are appropriately aggregated or disaggregated and clearly described, and related disclosures are relevant and understandable in the context of the requirements of the applicable financial reporting framework.

关于期末账户余额以及相关披露的认定

存在：记录的资产、负债和所有者权益是存在的。

权利和义务：记录的资产由被审计单位拥有或控制，记录的负债是被审计单位应当履行的偿还义务。

完整性：所有应当记录的资产、负债和所有者权益均已记录，并且所有与之相关的应当包括在财务报表中的披露均已包括。

准确性、计价和分摊：资产、负债和所有者权益以恰当的金额已包括在财务报表中，与之相关的计价或分摊调整已恰当记录，并且与之相关的披露已恰当计量和描述。

分类：所有资产、负债和所有者权益已记录于恰当的账户。

列报：所有资产、负债、所有者权益已经恰当地汇总或分解，并且清楚地表述，根据适用的财务报告框架，与之相关的披露是相关的和可理解的。

【学习提示】

两类认定有什么关系?

一般而言，与各类交易和事项相关的认定，通常涉及利润表项目的审计，比如营业收入的发生等；而与期末账户余额相关的认定，主要与资产负债表项目的审计相关，比如存货的存在；与列报相关的认定，表达的就是上述这两类认定如何在报表中列示的问题，比如关联交易的披露的完整性和准确性。

存在与完整性是方向相反的两个认定。以存货的审计为例，存在是指账面已经记录的存货是真实存在的，对于审计人员而言，验证时应该从存货账面记录追查至存货的实物资产；而完整性则是指企业所有应当记录的存货都已经入账，因此审计时应当从实物资产追查至账面记录。发生与完整性有同样的关系。

D-2 Audit Evidence / 审计证据

Audit Evidence

Audit evidence is all of the information used by the auditor in arriving at the conclusions on the auditor's opinion is based. Audit evidence includes both information contained in the accounting records underlying the financial statements and information obtained from other sources.

审计证据

审计证据是指审计人员为了得出审计结论、形成审计意见而使用的所有信息。审计证据既包括形成财务报表的会计记录中的各种信息，也包括其他来源的信息。

审计人员必须在每项审计工作中获取充分适当的审计证据，以满足发表审计意见的要求。

Sufficient and Appropriate Audit Evidence

The appropriateness of audit evidence is the measure of the quality of it, that is, its relevance and its reliability in providing support for the conclusions on which the auditor's opinion is based.

The sufficiency of audit evidence is the measure of the quantity of audit evidence. The quantity of audit evidence required is affected by the auditor's assessment of the risks of material misstatement and also by the quality of such audit evidence.

审计证据的充分性和适当性

审计证据的适当性，是对审计证据质量的衡量，即审计证据在支持审计意见所依据的结论方面具有相关性和可靠性。

相关性是指用作审计证据的信息与审计程序的目的和所考虑的相关认定之间的逻辑关系。审计证据的相关性可能受审计测试方向的影响。

可靠性是指证据的可信程度。审计证据的可靠性受其来源和性质的影响，并取决于获取审计证据的具体环境。

审计证据的充分性，是对审计证据数量的衡量。审计人员需要获取的审计证据的数量受其对重大错报风险评估的影响（评估的重大错报风险越高，需要的审计证据可能越多），并受审计证据质量的影响（审计证据质量越高，需要的审计证据可能越少）。

D－3 Audit Procedures / 审计程序

Audit Procedures

Auditors obtain evidence by one or more of the following procedures: inspection of tangible assets, inspection of documentation or records, observation, inquiry, confirmation, recalculation, reperformance, analytical procedures.

审计程序

在审计过程中，审计人员可根据需要单独或综合运用以下审计程序，以获取充分适当的审计证据：检查有形资产、检查书面记录或文件、观察、询问、函证、重新计算、重新执行和分析程序。

Inspection

Inspection involvcs examining records or documents, whether internal or external, in paper form, electronic form, or other media, or a physical examination of an asset. Inspection of records and documents provides audit evidence of varying degrees of reliability, depending on their nature and source and, in the case of internal records and documents, on the effectiveness of the controls over their production.

Inspection of tangible assets may provide reliable audit evidence with respect to their existence, but not necessarily about the entity's rights and obligations or the valuation of the assets. Inspection of individual inventory items may accompany the observation of inventory counting.

检查

检查是指审计人员对客户内部或外部生成的，以纸质、电子或其他介质形式存在的记录或文件进行审查，或者对实物资产进行检查。检查文件或记录可以提供可靠程度不同的审计证据，审计证据的可靠性取决于记录或文件的性质和来源。对于内部记录或文件，其可靠性则取决于生成该记录或文件的内部控制的有效性。

实地检查账面记录的有形资产，可为其存在提供可靠的审计证据，但不一定能够为权利和义务或计价等认定提供可靠证据。检查存货资产时，通常还伴随着观察存货盘点这项审计程序。

检查某些文件可以提供有关资产存在的直接证据，比如构成金融工具的一些文件，但是检查此类文件并不一定能提供有关所有权或计价的审计证据。

Observation

Observation consists of looking at a process or procedure being performed by others, for example, the auditor's observation of inventory counting by the entity's personnel, or of the performance of control activities. Observation provides audit evidence about the performance of a process or procedure, but is limited to the point in time at which the observation takes place, and by the fact that the act of being observed may affect how the process or procedure is performed.

观察

观察是指审计人员察看相关人员正在从事的活动或实施的程序，比如对客户的存货盘点或是控制活动的表现进行观察。观察可以提供执行有关过程或程序的审计证据，但其提供的审计证据是有限的。因为该程序所提供的证据仅限于观察发生的时点，并且被观察人员的行为也可能因为被观察而受影响。

Inquiry

Inquiry consists of seeking information of knowledgeable persons, both financial and non-financial, within the entity or outside the entity. Inquiries may range from formal written inquiries to informal oral inquiries. Strength of evidence depends on the knowledge and integrity of source of information. Inquiry alone does not provide sufficient audit evidence to detect material misstatement at assertion level, nor is sufficient to test the operating effectiveness of controls.

询问

询问是指审计人员以书面或口头方式，向客户内部或外部的知情人员（包括财务人员和非财务人员）获取有关信息。该项程序所提供的证据的证明力取决于信息提供者的诚信以及学识。仅仅依靠询问这项程序，不足以提供充分适当的证据来验证某个认定是否存在重大错报，以及某项内部控制的运行是否有效。

External Confirmation

An external confirmation represents audit evidence obtained by the auditor as a direct written response to the auditor from a third party (the confirming party), in paper form, or by electronic or other medium.

When confirmation is undertaken, the method of requesting information from the customer may be either positive or negative.

函证

函证是指审计人员直接从第三方（被询证者）获取书面答复，以验证某信息的准确性。书面答复可以采用纸质、电子或其他介质等形式。例如，审计人员可以向银行函证客户银行存款的余额。

函证有两种方式：积极的函证方式与消极的函证方式。

Positive Confirmation Request

A positive confirmation request is a request that the confirming party responds directly to the auditor indicating whether the confirming party agrees or disagrees with the information in the request, or providing the requested information.

积极的函证方式

如果采用积极的函证方式,审计人员应当要求被询证者无论是否同意询证函所列示的信息,都必须回函,或填列询证函所要求的信息。

Negative Confirmation Request

A negative confirmation request is a request that the confirming party responds directly to the auditor only if the confirming party disagrees with the information provided in the request.

消极的函证方式

如果采用消极的函证方式,审计人员只要求被询证者仅在不同意询证函列示信息的情况下才予以回函。

【学习提示】

如何选择积极的或消极的函证方式?

函证是一项非常重要的审计程序,在审计应收账款时,审计人员应当实施函证程序,除非有充分证据表明应收账款对财务报表不重要,或函证很可能无效。如果不对应收账款进行函证，审计人员应当在审计工作底稿中说明理由。除此以外，函证还可以用于银行存款、应付账款或由第三方代为保管的存货等项目的审计。

在两种函证方式中，积极的函证方式可以提供更为可靠的证据，因此只有在重大错报风险评估水平较低、涉及大量余额较小的账户、预期不存在大量的错报，并且没有理由相信被询证者不认真对待函证的时候，才可以采用消极的函证方式。在实务中，审计人员可以将两种方式结合使用。比如，审计人员可以对所有的或抽取的大额的账户余额采用积极的函证方式，而对抽取的小额的账户采用消极的函证方式。

Recalculation

Recalculation consists of checking the mathematical accuracy of documents or records. Recalculation may be performed manually or electronically.

重新计算

重新计算是指审计人员对记录或文件中的数据计算的准确性进行核对。重新计算可以通过人工方式或电子方式进行。

Reperformance

Reperformance involves the auditor’s independent execution of procedures or controls that were originally performed as part of the entity’s internal control.

重新执行

重新执行是指审计人员独立执行原本作为客户内部控制组成

部分的程序或控制。

Analytical Procedures

Analytical procedures consist of evaluations of financial information through analysis of plausible relationships among both financial and non-financial data. Analytical procedures also encompass investigation of identified fluctuations or relationships that are inconsistent with other relevant information or that differ from expected values by a significant amount.

Analytical procedures include the consideration of comparisons of the entity's financial information with, for example:

- Comparable information for prior periods.
- Anticipated results of the entity, such as budgets or forecasts, or expectations of the auditor, such as an estimation of depreciation.
- Similar industry information, such as a comparison of the entity's ratio of sales to accounts receivable with industry averages or with other entities of comparable size in the same industry.

Analytical procedures also include consideration of relationships, for example:

- Among elements of financial information that would be expected to conform to a predictable pattern based on the entity's experience, such as gross margin percentages.
- Between financial information and relevant non-financial information, such as payroll costs to number of employees.

分析程序

分析程序，是指审计人员通过分析不同财务数据之间以及财务数据与非财务数据之间的内在关系，对财务信息做出评价。分析程序还包括在必要时对识别出的、与其他相关信息不一致或与预期值差异重大的波动或关系进行调查。

在实施分析程序时，审计人员应当考虑将被审计单位的财务信息与下列各项信息进行比较：

- 以前期间的可比信息。
- 被审计单位的预期结果或者审计人员的预期数据。
- 可比的行业信息，比如将被审计单位的销售收入与应收账款的比率和行业平均数或同行业中规模相近的其他单位进行比较。

在实施分析程序时，审计人员还应当考虑下列关系：

- 财务信息各构成要素之间的关系，根据被审计单位的经验，预期这种关系符合某种可预测的规律，如毛利率。
- 财务信息与相关非财务信息之间的关系，如工资费用和员工人数之间的关系。

【学习提示】

财务报表认定、审计证据和审计程序之间是什么关系？

财务报表认定、审计证据和审计程序之间是有逻辑联系的。在审计时，我们首先必须明确审计的具体目标，也就是需要验证财务报表哪一项认定，然后再分析应该收集什么样的证据来达到目标，而获取证据的方法就是我们所说的审计程序。比如，我们希望验证期末资产负债表中的存货是真实存在的，那就必须取得实物证据，这就要求审计人员在期末实地检查客户的存货；如果我们的目标是验证这些存货是属于客户的资产，那么通过观察存货盘点取得的证据显然是不够的。因此，我们就必须检查有关存货的所有权凭证，比如购货发票等。所以，在学习各个循环的审计程序时，必须从财务报表的认定出发，这样可以帮助我们更好地理解各项审计程序的意义。

D－4 Audit Sampling / 审计抽样

Audit Sampling

Audit sampling (sampling) is the application of audit procedures to less than 100% of items within a population of audit relevance such that all sampling units have a chance of selection in order to provide the auditor with a reasonable basis on which to draw conclusions about the entire population.

Population — The entire set of data from which a sample is selected and about which the auditor wishes to draw conclusions.

审计抽样

审计抽样（即抽样），是指审计人员对具有审计相关性的总体中低于100%的项目实施审计程序，使所有抽样单元都有被选取的机会，为审计人员针对整个总体得出结论提供合理基础。

总体是指审计人员从中选取样本并期望据此得出结论的整个数据集合。

审计抽样应当具备三个特征：

1. 对某类交易或账户余额中低于100%的项目实施审计程序；

2. 所有抽样单元都有被选取的机会；

3. 可以根据样本项目的测试结果推断出有关抽样总体的结论。

【学习提示】

所有审计程序中都必须使用审计抽样吗？

随着企业规模的扩大和经营复杂程度的不断上升，在审计中对每一笔交易进行检查变得既不可行也无必要。审计抽样技术的发展，可以帮助审计人员在合理的时间内以合理的成本获得充分、适当的审计证据，得出审计结论。但是，我们也要注意，审计抽样并非在所有审计程序中都可使用。比如，当审计人员通过实施询问、观察等审计程序，以获取有关控制运行有效性的审计证据时，就不宜使用审计抽样。另外，在实施实质性分析程序时，审计人员也不宜使用审计抽样。

Statistical or Non-statistical Sampling

Statistical sampling is an approach to sampling that has the following characteristics：

(a) Random selection of samples；and

(b) Probability theory to evaluate sample results，including measurement of sampling risk.

Any approach that does not have both these characteristics is considered to be non-statistical sampling.

统计抽样和非统计抽样

在运用审计抽样时，审计人员可以根据自己的职业判断，选择使用统计抽样或者非统计抽样方法。统计抽样是指同时具备下列特征的抽样方法：

1. 随机选取样本项目；

2. 运用概率论评价样本结果，包括量化抽样风险。

不同时具备上述两个特征的抽样方法为非统计抽样。

也就是说，在随机选样的情况下，如果审计人员没有运用概率论评价样本结果；或者，审计人员在非随机选样的情况下抽样，这些都是非统计抽样。

统计抽样的优点在于能够客观地计量抽样风险，并通过调整样本规模精确地控制风险，定量评价样本结果。另外，统计抽样还有助于审计人员更高效地设计样本，计量所获取的证据的充分性。但是统计抽样可能发生额外的成本。非统计抽样只要设计适当，也能提供与统计抽样同样有效的效果。

Sampling Risk

Sampling risk is the risk that the auditor's conclusion based on a sample may be different from the conclusion if the entire population was subjected to the same audit procedure.

Sampling risk can lead to two types of erroneous conclusions:

(a) In the case of a test of controls, that controls are more effective than they actually are, or in the case of a test of details, that a material misstatement does not exist when in fact it does. The auditor is primarily concerned with this type of erroneous conclusion because it affects audit effectiveness and is more likely to lead to an inappropriate audit opinion.

(b) In the case of a test of controls, that controls are less effective than they actually are, or in the case of a test of details, that a material misstatement exists when in fact it does not. This type of erroneous conclusion affects audit efficiency as it would usually lead to additional work to establish that initial conclusions were incorrect.

抽样风险

抽样风险，是指审计人员根据样本得出的结论，可能不同于对整个总体实施与样本相同的审计程序所得出的结论的风险。抽样风险与样本规模和抽样方法有关。

抽样风险可能导致以下两类错误结论：

1. 在控制测试中，审计人员评估的内部控制的有效性高于其实际有效性；在细节测试中，审计人员推断某一重大错报不存在而实际上存在。审计人员主要关注这类错误的结论，因为它们不仅会影响审计效果，并且可能导致错误的审计意见。

2. 在控制测试中，审计人员评估的内部控制的有效性低于其实际有效性；在细节测试中，审计人员推断某一重大错报存在而实际上不存在。这类错误通常会影响审计效率，因为为了推翻原来错误的结论，往往需要执行额外的审计工作。

Non-sampling Risk

Non-sampling risk is the risk that the auditor reaches an erroneous conclusion for any reason not related to sampling risk.

非抽样风险

非抽样风险，是指审计人员由于任何与抽样风险无关的原因而得出错误结论的风险。即使审计人员对某类交易或账户余额的所有项目都实施审计程序，也可能未发现重大错报或控制失效。

【学习提示】

如何控制抽样风险与非抽样风险?

只要在审计中运用了抽样技术,就一定会存在抽样风险。抽样风险与样本规模呈反向变动:样本规模越小,抽样风险越大;样本规模越大,抽样风险越小。审计人员可以通过扩大样本规模来降低抽样风险。如果对总体中所有的项目都实施检查,就不存在抽样风险,此时审计风险完全由非抽样风险产生。

而非抽样风险与样本规模无关。导致非抽样风险的原因主要如下:

1. 总体与审计测试的目标无关;
2. 未能适当定义误差;
3. 审计程序的选择不适当;
4. 未能适当评价审计发现;
5. 其他。

审计人员无法量化非抽样风险,只能通过审计质量控制政策和程序,对审计工作进行更适当的指导、监督和复核,更仔细地设计审计程序,从而将非抽样风险降低至可以接受的水平。

Methods of Selecting Samples

The main methods of selecting samples are random selection, systematic selection, haphazard selection, block selection, monetary selection.

Random selection applied through random number generators, for example, random number tables.

Systematic selection, in which the number of sampling units in the population is divided by the sample size to give a sampling interval, for example 50, and having determined a starting point within the first 50, each 50th sampling unit thereafter is selected.

Monetary unit sampling is a type of value-weighted selection in which sample size, selection and evaluation results in a conclusion in monetary amounts.

Haphazard selection, in which the auditor selects the sample without following a structured technique. Although no structured technique is used, the auditor would nonetheless avoid any conscious bias or predictability and thus attempt to ensure that all items in the population have a chance of selection. Haphazard selection is not appropriate when using statistical sampling.

Block selection involves selection of a block(s) of contiguous items from within the population.

选样的方法

选取样本的基本方法有随机数表选样、系统选样、随意选样、整群选样和货币单元选样。

随机数表选样是指使用随机数表来选样的方法。

审计人员可以使用计算机生成随机数，随机数是一组从长期来看出现概率相同的数码。随机数表也称乱数表，它是由随机生成的从0～9共10个数字组成的数表。每个数字在表中出现的次数大致相同，它们出现在表中的顺序是随机的。随机数表选样需要首先对总体项目进行编号，然后确定选样的起点与路线，依次查找符合总体项目编号要求的数字，即为选中的号码，与此号码相对应的总体项目即为选取的样本项目。随机数表选样能够确保总体中每个抽样单元被选取的概率相等。

系统选样，也称等距选样，是指按照相同的间隔从审计对象总体中等距离地选取样本的一种方法。使用系统选样，首先用总体规模除以样本规模，计算选样间隔，如果选样间隔确定为50，那么在第一个选样间隔中选取一个作为选样起点，然后每隔50个单元，就是选中的样本。比如，选样起点的号码为669，则第二个被选中的样本就是719(669+50)号，依次类推。

货币单元选样是加权选样的一种，在该方法下，样本规模、选样和评估结果都以货币金额来表示。由于总体中的每个货币单元被选中的机会相同，所以总体中某一项目被选中的概率等于该项目的金额与总体金额的比率。项目金额越大，被选中的概率就越大。这种选样方法有助于审计人员将审计重点放在金额较大的项目，更容易发现那些高估的错报。

随意选样，在这种选样方法中，审计人员选取样本不采用结构化的方法。但是为了保证总体中所有项目都有被选中的机会，审计人员应该避免任何有意识的偏向或可预见性。它属于非随机基础选样方法，随意选样不能在统计抽样中使用，只适用于非统计抽样。

整群选样或者连续选样，是指从总体中选取一组连续的样本。比如，审计人员可以抽取50张连续编号的支票，以验证是否有相关负责人签字。这种选样方法可能导致所选取的样本缺乏代表性，因此在审计测试中并不常见。

Anomaly

Anomaly is a misstatement or deviation that is demonstrably not representative of misstatements or deviations in a population.

异常误差

异常误差，是指对总体中的错报或偏差明显不具有代表性的错报或偏差。审计人员应当获取充分适当的审计证据，以确保该误差对总体不具有代表性。

Stratification

Stratification — The process of dividing a population into sub-populations, each of which is a group of sampling units which have similar characteristics (often monetary value).

分层

分层是指将总体划分为多个子总体的过程，每个子总体由一组具有相同特征(通常为货币金额)的抽样单元组成。

分层使具有相同特征的个体样本被包含在一个层中，从而降低了层内样本的个体变异性，达到减少样本规模、提高审计效率的目的。这种方法主要适用于总体项目存在重大变异性的抽样。比如，在审计应收账款时，我们可以根据应收账款明细账期末余额的大小，将应收账款进行分层。

Tolerable Misstatement

Tolerable Misstatement — A monetary amount set by the auditor in respect of which the auditor seeks to obtain an appropriate level of assurance that the monetary amount set by the auditor is not exceeded by the actual misstatement in the population.

可容忍错报

可容忍错报是指审计人员设定的货币金额，审计人员试图对总体中实际错报不超过该货币金额获取适当水平的保证。

Tolerable Rate of Deviation

Tolerable Rate of Deviation — A rate of deviation from prescribed internal control procedures set by the auditor in respect of which the auditor seeks to obtain an appropriate level of assurance that the rate of deviation set by the auditor is not exceeded by the actual rate of deviation in the population.

可容忍偏差率

可容忍偏差率，是指审计人员设定的偏离规定的内部控制程序的比率，审计人员试图对总体中的实际偏差率不超过该比率获取适当水平的保证。

实际上，可容忍偏差率就是审计人员能够接受的最大偏差数量，如果偏差超过这一数量，审计人员就会降低对内部控制程序的信赖。

【学习提示】

可容忍错报与重要性有什么关联？

可容忍错报意味着总体中的错报只要不超过这个设定水平，审计人员仍然接受“总体不存在重大错报”的结论。那么，可容忍错报与重要性有什么关联呢？事实上，可容忍错报就是实际执行的重要性水平在特定抽样程序中的运用。可容忍错报可能等于或低于实际执行的重要性。

我们可以把可容忍偏差率与可容忍错报统称为可容忍误差。也就是审计人员在认为测试目标已实现的情况下，准备接受的总体最大误差。在控制测试中，它就是可容忍偏差率；在细节测试中，它就是可容忍错报。

Projected Misstatements

Projected misstatements are the auditor's best estimate of misstatements in populations, involving the projection of misstatements identified in audit samples to the entire populations from which the samples were drawn.

推断错报

推断错报是指审计人员对总体存在的错报做出的最佳估计数，涉及根据在审计样本中识别出的错报来推断总体的错报。推断错报通常是指通过测试样本估计出的总体的错报减去在测试中发现的已经识别的具体错报。

【学习提示】

1. 在抽样过程中，如何推断总体错报？

在抽样过程中，推断总体错报的方式有很多种，如比率法、差异法等。比率法即用样本中的错报金额除以样本中包含的账面金额占总体账面总金额的比例。例如，审计人员选取的样本的金额合计是总体总金额的10%（样本金额÷总体金额＝10%），经审计，审计人员发现错报为10万元，则总体错报的最佳估计数为100万元（10÷10%）。其中已经识别的错报是10万元，推断的错报是90万元。

2. 如何进行审计抽样？

审计抽样的主要步骤可总结如下：

(1) 确定测试目标和总体特征。

正确确定测试目标才能确保总体的适当和完整。例如，在细节测试中，审计人员的目标是测试销售收入的发生，则总体可以定义为销售收入明细账；如果测试目标是销售收入的完整性，则将被审计单位的出库单、销售发票作为总体就更适当。

(2) 确定样本规模。

样本规模主要受可接受的抽样风险、可容忍的误差(可容忍偏差率或者可容忍错报)、预计总体误差、总体变异性以及总体规模等因素的影响。

(3) 确定选样的方法。

审计人员应当根据需要选择随机选样、系统选样、随意选样等方法来抽取样本。然后对样本实施审计程序。

(4) 推断总体误差，评价样本结果。

审计人员应该根据样本误差，推断总体误差。对控制测试而言，就是根据样本中发现的偏差率推断总体偏差率；在细节测试中，就是根据样本中发现的错报金额推断总体错报金额。然后审计人员应当将总体误差与可容忍误差做比较，评价抽样结果。如果总体误差低于可容忍误差，则总体可以接受，否则总体不能接受。

D-5 Computer-assisted Audit Techniques / 计算机辅助审计技术

Computer-assisted Audit Techniques

Computer-assisted audit techniques (CAAT) are the applications of auditing procedures using the computer as an audit tool. The two most commonly used CAATs are **audit software** and **test data.**

计算机辅助审计技术

计算机辅助审计技术，是指利用计算机和相关软件作为审计工具来执行审计程序。最常用的计算机辅助审计技术有两种：审计软件和测试数据。

Audit Software

Audit software consists of computer programs used by the auditors, as part of their auditing procedures, to process data of audit significance from the entity's accounting system. Audit software is used for substantive procedures.

审计软件

审计软件是指审计人员使用计算机程序处理来自客户会计系统的具有审计价值的数据。审计软件主要适用于实质性程序。

比如，审计人员可以利用审计软件帮助自己分析应收账款的账龄，然后选择适当的样本进行函证。

Test Data

Test data techniques are used in conducting audit procedures by entering data into an entity's computer system, and comparing the results obtained with pre-determined results. Test data is used for tests of controls.

测试数据

测试数据是指审计人员将自己设计的一组数据输入客户的计算机系统中，然后将运行结果与预先设定的结果做比较。测试数据主要用于验证系统的内部控制的有效性。比如，客户的订货系统的流程是，客户先输入订货信息，然后系统自动生成出库单。针对这项内部控制，审计人员可以输入一组订货信息，测试订货系统是否会自动生成出库单、出库单上的信息是否与所输入的订货信息一致。

Auditing Around the Computer

Auditing around the computer means that the 'internal' software of the computer is not documented or audited by the auditor, but the inputs to the computer are agreed to the expected outputs from the computer.

绕过计算机审计

绕过计算机审计意味着审计人员没有记录和审计计算机内部的软件，而只是把输入计算机的信息与预计的输出结果进行比较。在这种审计方法下，不可以直接测试计算机系统的工作过程，一旦发生错误，也很难找出错误发生的原因，因此会导致审计风险的增加。

D-6 The Work of Others / 其他人的工作

Using the Work of Internal Audit

The objectives of the external auditor, where the entity has an internal audit function and the external auditor expects to use the work of the function to modify the nature or timing, or reduce the extent, of audit procedures to be performed directly by the external auditor, or to use internal auditors to provide direct assistance, are:

(a) To determine whether the work of the internal audit

function or direct assistance from internal auditors can be used, and if so, in which areas and to what extent;

(b) If using the work of the internal audit function, to determine whether that work is adequate for purposes of the audit; and

(c) If using internal auditors to provide direct assistance, to appropriately direct, supervise and review their work.

利用内部审计人员的工作

当客户有内部审计职责，而审计人员希望通过利用内部审计职能来改变由他们直接执行的审计程序的性质、时间或者缩减审计程序的范围时，或者利用内部审计人员提供直接协助时，外部审计人员的目标是：

1. 确定是否能够利用内部审计职责的工作或者内部审计人员的直接协助，如果可以利用，则需要确定在哪些领域、在多大程度上可以利用；

2. 如果需要利用内部审计职责，则应当确定该工作是否足以实现审计的目标；

3. 如果需要内部审计人员提供直接协助，则应当确定如何对他们的工作进行适当的指导、监督和复核。

Internal Audit Function

The internal audit function is a function of an entity that performs assurance and consulting activities designed to evaluate and improve the effectiveness of the entity's governance, risk management and internal control processes.

内部审计职责

内部审计职责是指由被审计单位开展的一项保证和咨询活动，目的是评价和改善公司治理、风险管理和内部控制的有效性。

Evaluating the Internal Audit Function

The external auditor shall determine whether the work of the internal audit function can be used for purposes of the audit by evaluating the following:

(a) The extent to which the internal audit function's organizational status and relevant policies and procedures support the objectivity of the internal auditors;

(b) The level of competence of the internal audit function; and

(c) Whether the internal audit function applies a systematic and disciplined approach, including quality control.

评估内部审计职责

外部审计人员在评估内部审计人员的工作是否可以实现审计目标时，需要考虑以下几个因素：

1. 内部审计人员的组织地位和相关的政策及程序是否足够支持内部审计人员的客观性；

2. 内部审计职责的胜任能力；

3. 内部审计职责是否运用了系统规范的方法，包括质量控制。

【学习提示】

外部审计人员如何评价内部审计人员的工作?

当外部审计人员确定要利用内部审计人员的工作时，应该

评价内部审计人员的客观性。所谓内部审计人员的客观性，也就是内部审计人员可以不带偏见、不受干扰地执行任务。外部审计人员应当通过内部审计的组织地位，即内部审计向哪个级别的治理层或管理层负责，来评价内部审计的客观性。在评价内部审计人员的胜任能力时，主要考虑他们的职业资格、职业经验以及技术培训等。在评价内部审计职责的工作方法时，主要考虑：内部审计活动是否经过适当的计划、监督、复核和记录，是否收集了充分适当的证据以得出合理的结论；内部审计人员得出的结论是否恰当，编制的报告是否与已执行的工作结果一致。

Direct Assistance

Direct Assistance — The use of internal auditors to perform audit procedures under the direction, supervision and review of the external auditor.

The external auditor shall not use an internal auditor to provide direct assistance if:

(a) There are significant threats to the objectivity of the internal auditor; or

(b) The internal auditor lacks sufficient competence to perform the proposed work.

The external auditor shall not use internal auditors to provide direct assistance to perform procedures that:

(a) Involve making significant judgments in the audit;

(b) Relate to higher assessed risks of material misstatement where the judgment required in performing the relevant audit procedures or evaluating the audit evidence gathered is more than limited;

(c) Relate to work with which the internal auditors have been involved;

(d) Relate to decisions the external auditor makes regarding the internal audit function and the use of its work or direct assistance.

直接协助

直接协助是指在外部审计人员的指导、监督和复核下，利用内部审计人员执行审计程序。

当存在下列情况时，外部审计人员不应该由内部审计人员提供直接协助：

1. 内部审计人员的客观性有重大的威胁；

2. 内部审计人员缺乏执行相关工作的胜任能力。

执行下列程序时，外部审计人员不应该由内部审计人员提供直接协助：

1. 审计中涉及重大判断的项目；

2. 重大错报风险的估计水平较高，而且在确定审计程序和评估审计证据时需要更多判断的项目（比如审计人员可以让内部审计人员帮助检查应收账款账龄的准确性，但是在评估坏账准备的准确性时，不得由内部审计人员提供直接协助）；

3. 涉及内部审计人员自己的工作；

4. 外部审计人员做出的有关内部审计职责、利用内部审计的工作或内部审计提供直接协助的决策。

Using the Work of an Auditor's Expert

Auditor's Expert — An individual or organization possessing expertise in a field other than accounting or auditing, whose work in that field is used by the auditor to assist the auditor in obtaining sufficient appropriate audit evidence. An auditor's expert may be either an auditor's internal expert (who is a partner or staff, including temporary staff, of the auditor's firm or a network firm), or an auditor's external expert.

Management's Expert — An individual or organization possessing expertise in a field other than accounting or auditing, whose work in that field is used by the entity to assist the entity in preparing the financial statements.

利用专家的工作

审计人员的专家,是指在会计或审计以外的某一领域具有专长的个人或组织,并且其工作被审计人员利用,以协助审计人员获取充分、适当的审计证据。专家既可能是会计师事务所的内部专家(如会计师事务所或其网络事务所的合伙人或员工,包括临时员工),也可能是会计师事务所的外部专家。

管理层的专家,是指在会计、审计以外的某一领域具有专长的个人或组织,其工作被管理层利用,以协助编制财务报表。

The Competence, Capabilities and Objectivity of the Auditor's Expert

The auditor shall evaluate whether the auditor's expert has the necessary competence, capabilities and objectivity for the auditor's purposes. In the case of an auditor's external expert, the evaluation of objectivity shall include inquiry regarding interests and relationships that may create a threat to that expert's objectivity.

评价专家的胜任能力、专业素质和客观性

审计人员应该评价专家是否具备为实现审计目的而必要的胜任能力、专业素质和客观性。如果是外部专家，还应当询问专家与被审计单位之间是否有会威胁专家的客观性的利益或其他关系。

Evaluating the Adequacy of the Auditor's Expert's Work

The auditor shall evaluate the adequacy of the auditor's expert's work for the auditor's purposes, including:

(a) The relevance and reasonableness of that expert's findings or conclusions, and their consistency with other audit evidence;

(b) If that expert's work involves use of significant assumptions and methods, the relevance and reasonableness of those assumptions and methods in the circumstances; and

(c) If that expert's work involves the use of source data that is significant to that expert's work, the relevance, completeness, and accuracy of that source data.

评价专家工作的恰当性

审计人员应当评价专家的工作是否足以实现审计的目的，主要考虑：

1. 专家的工作结果或结论的相关性与合理性，以及与其他审计证据的一致性；

2. 如果专家的工作涉及使用重要的假设和方法，就考虑这些假设和方法在具体情况下的相关性和合理性；

3. 如果专家的工作涉及使用重要的原始数据，就考虑这些原始数据的相关性、完整性和准确性。

Service Organization

Service Organization — A third party organization (or segment of a third party organization) that provides services to user entities that are part of those entities' information systems relevant to financial reporting.

服务机构

服务机构是指向被审计单位提供服务，并且其服务构成与被审计单位财务报告相关的信息系统组成部分的第三方机构(或第三方机构的组成部分)。

Service Auditor

Service Auditor — An auditor who, at the request of the service organization, provides an assurance report on the controls of a service organization.

服务机构的审计人员

服务机构的审计人员是指接受服务机构的委托，为服务机构的控制出具鉴证报告的审计人员。

User Entity

User Entity — An entity that uses a service organization

and whose financial statements are being audited.

使用服务机构的单位

使用服务机构的单位，是指使用服务机构且其财务报表正在接受审计的实体。

User Auditor

User Auditor — An auditor who audits and reports on the financial statements of a user entity.

使用服务机构的单位的审计人员

使用服务机构的单位的审计人员，是指对使用服务机构的单位的财务报表进行审计的审计人员。

Service Organization's System

Service Organization's System — The policies and procedures designed, implemented and maintained by the service organization to provide user entities with the services covered by the service auditor's report.

服务机构的系统

服务机构的系统，是指为了向被审计单位提供服务机构审计人员的报告所涵盖的服务而由服务机构设计、执行和维护的政策和程序。

Subservice Organization

Subservice Organization — A service organization used by another service organization to perform some of the services provided to user entities that are part of those user entities' information systems relevant to financial reporting.

分包服务机构

分包服务机构，是指为了向被审计单位提供服务而使用的另一个服务机构。其提供的服务是服务机构应提供服务的一部分，且构成被审计单位与财务报告相关的信息系统的组成部分。

Type 1 Report

Type 1 report is the report on the description and design of controls at a service organization. It comprises：

(a) A description，prepared by management of the service organization，of the service organization's system，control objectives and related controls that have been designed and implemented as at a specified date；and

(b) A report by the service auditor with the objective of conveying reasonable assurance that includes the service auditor's opinion on the description of the service organization's system，control objectives and related controls and the suitability of the design of the controls to achieve the specified control objectives.

第一类报告

第一类报告是指针对服务机构对控制的描述和设计出具的报告。它主要包括：

1. 由服务机构管理层对服务机构系统、控制目标以及在特定日期已得到设计和执行的相关控制的描述；

2. 由服务机构的审计人员出具的、旨在向使用者提供合理保证的报告，包括针对服务机构对系统、控制目标和相关控制的描述，以及控制的设计对于实现特定控制目标的适当性发表的意见。

Type 2 Report

Type 2 report is the report on the description, design, and operating effectiveness of controls at a service organization. It comprises:

(a) A description, prepared by management of the service organization, of the service organization's system, control objectives and related controls, their design and implementation as at a specified date or throughout a specified period and, in some cases, their operating effectiveness throughout a specified period; and

(b) A report by the service auditor with the objective of conveying reasonable assurance that includes:

a. The service auditor's opinion on the description of the service organization's system, control objectives and related controls, the suitability of the design of the controls to achieve the specified control objectives, and the operating effectiveness of the controls; and

b. A description of the service auditor's tests of the controls and the results thereof.

第二类报告

第二类报告是指针对服务机构对控制的描述和设计以及运行的有效性出具的报告。它主要包括：

1. 由服务机构的管理层做出的描述，涉及服务机构的系统、控制目标和相关控制，在特定日期或特定期间控制的设计和执行，以及在某些情况下控制在特定期间运行的有效性。

2. 由服务机构的审计人员出具的、旨在向使用者提供合理保证的报告，包括：

(1) 针对服务机构对系统、控制目标和相关控制的描述，以及控制的设计对于实现特定控制目标的适当性，以及控制运行的有效性发表的意见；

(2) 针对控制测试及其结果做出的描述。

【学习提示】

当审计人员确定要利用他人的工作时，如何评价他人的工作？

不论是利用内部审计的工作还是利用专家的工作，或者审计那些使用了服务机构工作的单位，审计人员主要面临两个问题：一是确定是否需要利用他人的工作；二是在确定需要利用他人的工作以后，应如何评价他们的工作。这时，审计人员首先需要评价他人的专业胜任能力以及客观性。在评价专家的胜任能力时，可以参考个人的从业经验、资格证书、职业团体或协会的会员资格、出版物或发表的论文等信息；在评价客观性时，可以参考审计独立性的评价方法，关注他人与被审计单位的各种关系是否会影响其客观公正的态度。然后，审计人员还需要进一步评价由他人所执行的特定工作，包括评价内部审计特定工作以及专家的特定工作。评价的重点是确定他们所执行的工作是否足以达到审计目的。

另外还需要注意，即使审计人员使用了他人的工作，但是在审计报告中一般不应该提及他人的工作，除非法律法规有特殊的要求。

Part E

Review and Reporting / 复核和报告

E－1 Subsequent Events / 期后事项

Subsequent Events

Subsequent events are events occurring between the date of the financial statements and the auditor's report, and facts that become known to the auditor after the date of the auditor's report.

There are two types of subsequent events:

Those that provide evidence of conditions that existed at the year-end date (adjusting events).

Those that are indicative of conditions that arose after the year-end date (non-adjusting events).

期后事项

期后事项是指财务报表日至审计报告之间发生的事项，以及审计人员在审计报告日后知悉的事实。

期后事项有两类：

一是对财务报表日已经存在的情况提供证据的事项，即调整事项。这类事项对财务报表日已经存在的情况提供了新的或进一步证据的事项。

二是表明财务报表日后发生的情况的事项，即非调整事项。这类事项对财务报表日后发生的情况提供证据，因此不需要调整财务报表。

【学习提示】

如何区分调整事项与非调整事项？

区分调整事项与非调整事项的关键是：调整事项是针对在财务报表日已经存在的情况，在财务报表日后有了新的证据，需要提请被审计单位管理层调整财务报表及与之相关的披露信息。而非调整事项的主要情况发生在财务报表日以后，因此不需要调整被审计单位的本期财务报表，但如果不披露相关信息，被审计单位的财务报表可能被误解，因此应该在财务报表中以附注形式予以适当披露。比如，财务报表日被审计单位认为可以收回的大额应收款项，因财务报表日后债务人破产而无法收回。事实上，债务人财务状况恶化的情况在资产负债表日已经存在，所以被审计单位应该增加计提坏账准备，调整财务报表有关项目的金额。但是，如果债务人在资产负债表日后是由于火灾导致了财务状况恶化，从而被审计单位无法收回应收账款。在这种情况下，债务人财务状况恶化的情况在资产负债表日并不存在，因此不属于调整事项。但是由于坏账金额巨大，被审计单位可以在财务报表的附注中披露该信息。

Date of the Financial Statements

The date of the financial statements is the date of the end of the latest period covered by the financial statements.

财务报表日

财务报表日是指财务报表涵盖的最近期间的截止日期。

Date of Approval of the Financial Statements

The date of approval of the financial statements is the date on which all the statements that comprise the financial statements, including the related notes, have been prepared and those with the recognized authority have asserted that they have taken responsibility for those financial statements.

财务报表批准日

财务报表批准日是指构成整套财务报表的所有报表，包括相关的附注，已编制完成，并且被审计单位的董事会、管理层或类似机构已经认可其对财务报表的责任的日期。

Date of the Auditor's Report

The auditor's report shall be dated no earlier than the date on which the auditor has obtained sufficient appropriate audit evidence on which to base the auditor's opinion on the financial statements.

The date of the auditor's report informs the user of the auditor's report that the auditor has considered the effect of events and transactions of which the auditor became aware and that occurred up to that date.

审计报告日

审计报告日不应早于审计人员获取充分、适当的审计证据，并在此基础上对财务报表形成审计意见的日期。

审计报告的日期向财务报表使用者表明,审计人员已考虑其知悉的、截止审计报告日发生的事项和交易的影响。

在实务中,审计报告日与财务报表批准日通常是相同的日期。

Date the Financial Statements are Issued

The date the financial statements are issued is the date that the auditor's report and audited financial statements are made available to third parties.

财务报表报出日

财务报表报出日是指审计报告和已审计财务报表提供给第三方的日期。

【学习提示】

1. 审计人员对不同期间期后事项的责任是什么?

明确财务报表日、财务报表批准日、审计报告日、财务报表报出日这几个重要日期,是为了区分审计人员对期后事项审计的责任。

(1) 财务报表日至审计报告日之间的期后事项

对于发生在财务报表日至审计报告日之间的期后事项,审计人员负有主动识别的责任(active duty)。审计人员应当设计和实施审计程序,获取充分、适当的审计证据,以确定所有在这段时间发生的、需要在财务报表中调整或披露的事项均已得到识别,并正确地进行了处理。

(2) 审计报告日至财务报表报出日之间的期后事项

审计报告日至财务报表报出日之间的期后事项,审计人员负有被动识别的责任(passive duty)。审计报告日后,审计人员没有义务针对财务报表实施任何审计程序,要主动识别这段时间的期后事项比较困难。但是,由于财务报表尚未报出,管理层有责任将发现的可能影响财务报表的事实告知审计人员。当然,审计人员不能忽略来自其他途径,比如媒体报道等的信息。

(3) 财务报表报出日之后的期后事项

财务报表报出日之后,审计人员没有义务识别这个时段的期后事项,审计人员没有义务针对财务报表实施任何审计程序,但是并不能排除审计人员通过其他获悉可能对财务报表产生重大影响的期后事项的可能性。

2. 如何确定期后事项对审计报告的影响?

对有关期后事项的审计,应当按照如下步骤进行:

第一步,判断该事项的性质,根据其特征确定其分类,是归属于调整事项还是非调整事项。

第二步,判断被审计单位的会计处理是否正确。审计人员需要设计相关的审计程序,以确定有关该事项的计量和账务处理是否正确。

第三步,如果审计人员确定被审计单位会计处理存在错误,就需要提请被审计单位修改会计报表,包括调整事项的调整和非调整事项的披露。

第四步,如果被审计单位拒绝修改会计报表,审计人员就根据事先确定的重要性水平,判断应当出具何种类型的审计报告。

E-2 Going Concern / 持续经营

Going Concern Assumption

Under the going concern assumption, an entity is viewed as

continuing in business for the foreseeable future. When the use of going concern assumption is appropriate, assets and liabilities are recorded on the basis that the entity will be able to realise its assets and discharge its liabilities in the normal course of business. General purpose financial statements are prepared on a going concern basis, unless management either intends to liquidate the entity or to cease opcrations, or has no realistic alternative but to do so. If the going concern basis is not appropriate, the financial statements are prepared on a break-up basis.

持续经营假设

持续经营假设是指假设企业在可预见的将来,其生产经营会继续经营下去,不会破产。在持续经营的前提下,企业可以在正常的经营过程中变现资产、清偿债务。通用目的的财务报表一般是在持续经营的基础上编制的,除非管理层计划将被审计单位予以清算或终止经营,或者除此之外没有其他现实可行的选择。如果企业不能持续经营,就应该在清算的基础上编制财务报表。

Responsibilities of the Auditor

The auditor's responsibility is to obtain sufficient appropriate audit evidence about the appropriateness of management's use of the going concern assumption in the preparation of the financial statements and to conclude whether there is a material uncertainty about the entity's ability to continue as a going concern.

This responsibility exists even if the financial reporting framework used in the preparation of the financial statements does not include an explicit requirement for management to make a specific assessment of the entity's ability to continue as a going concern.

审计人员的责任

关于持续经营假设，审计人员的责任是获取充分适当的审计证据，以评估管理层在编制和列报财务报表时运用持续经营假设的适当性，并就持续经营能力是否存在重大不确定性得出结论。

即使编制财务报表时采用的财务报告编制基础没有明确要求管理层对持续经营能力做出专门评估，审计人员的这种责任仍然存在。

【学习提示】

审计人员如何评估持续经营假设的适当性?

关于持续经营，审计人员的责任是对管理层评估的再评估。管理层应当定期对其持续经营能力做出分析和判断，确定以持续经营假设为基础编制财务报表的适当性。审计人员应当评价管理层针对持续经营能力做出的评估。

考虑持续经营假设是否适当时，应按如下步骤进行：

第一步，审计人员应当结合风险评估程序，从财务、经营和其他方面识别是否存在可能导致对被审计单位持续经营能力产生重大疑虑的事项或情况。

第二步，如果识别出可能导致对持续经营能力产生重大疑虑的事项或情况，审计人员应当通过实施追加的审计程序，获取充分、适当的审计证据，以确定是否存在重大不确定性。

第三步，确定对审计报告的影响。

1. 如果被审计单位运用持续经营假设是适当的，但存在重大不确定性，且财务报表对重大不确定性已做出充分披露，审计人员应当发表无保留意见，并在审计报告中增加以“与持续经营相关的重大不确定性”为标题的单独部分，以提醒投资者关注这一事项。

2. 如果财务报表已经按照持续经营假设编制，但根据判断，审计人员认为管理层在财务报表中运用持续经营假设是不适当的，审计人员就应当发表否定意见。

3. 如果运用持续经营假设是适当的，但存在重大不确定性，且财务报表对重大不确定性未做出充分披露，审计人员应当根据对财务报表的影响程度，发表保留意见或否定意见。

E-3 Written Representations / 书面声明

Written Representations

Written representation is a written statement by management provided to the auditor to confirm certain matters or to support other audit evidence. Written representations in this context do not include financial statements, the assertions therein, or supporting books and records.

书面声明

书面声明是指管理层向审计人员提供的书面陈述，用以确认某些事项或支持其他审计证据。书面声明不包括财务报表及其认定，以及支持性账簿和相关记录。

Written Representations About Management's Responsibilities

Preparation of the Financial Statements

The auditor shall request management to provide a written

representation that it has fulfilled its responsibility for the preparation of the financial statements in accordance with the applicable financial reporting framework, including, where relevant, their fair presentation, as set out in the terms of the audit engagement.

Information Provided and Completeness of Transactions

The auditor shall request management to provide a written representation that:

(a) It has provided the auditor with all relevant information and access as agreed in the terms of the audit engagement;

(b) All transactions have been recorded and are reflected in the financial statements.

针对管理层责任的书面声明

针对**财务报表的编制**,审计人员应当要求管理层提供书面声明,确认其根据审计业务约定条款,履行了按照适用的财务报告编制基础,编制财务报表并使其实现公允反映的责任。

针对**提供的信息和交易的完整性**,审计人员应当要求管理层就下列事项提供书面声明:

1. 按照审计业务约定条款,已向审计人员提供所有相关信息,并允许审计人员不受限制地接触所有相关信息;

2. 所有交易均已记录并反映在财务报表中。

Other Written Representations

If, in addition to such required representations, the auditor determines that it is necessary to obtain one or more written representations to support other audit evidence relevant to the financial statements or one or more specific assertions in the financial statements, the auditor shall request such other written representations.

其他书面声明

除了所要求的声明之外，如果审计人员认为有必要获取一项或多项其他书面声明，以支持与财务报表或者与财务报表中的一项或多项具体认定相关的其他审计证据，审计人员应当要求管理层提供这些书面声明。

【学习提示】

1. 审计人员是否需要管理层提供其他书面声明？

除了审计准则明确要求的书面声明之外，审计人员应当运用职业判断确定何时需要管理层提供其他书面声明，以及需要什么样的书面声明。一般而言，在获取有关管理层的判断和意图的证据时，或者在对判断和意图进行评价时，审计人员可能认为有必要要求管理层提供特定的书面声明。比如在审计投资项目的时候，由于管理层的意图对投资的计价模式非常重要，而审计人员又无法从其他途径获得相关证据，这时，管理层的声明书就成为一项必要的审计证据。其他需要获取书面声明的情况主要包括：

(1) 管理层已经披露了所有已知的影响财务报表的舞弊指控或舞弊嫌疑的信息；

(2) 管理层已经披露了所有已知的、在编制财务报表时应当考虑其影响的违反或涉嫌违反法律法规的信息；

(3) 未更正错报单独或汇总对财务报表的影响是不重要的；

(4) 所有需要调整的期后事项都已经调整，所有需要披露的期后事项都已经披露；

(5) 管理层已经将所有已知的内部控制的缺陷告知审计人员；

(6) 做出会计估计时运用的重大假设是合理的；

(7) 其他。

2. 管理层书面声明的性质是什么？

书面声明是审计人员在财务报表审计中需要获取的必要信息，是审计证据的重要来源。如果管理层没有提供审计人员要求的书面声明，审计人员就需要提高警觉性。尤其是当管理层拒绝提供有关针对管理层责任的书面声明，包括针对财务报表的编制或者针对提供的信息和交易的完整性的书面声明时，审计人员应当对财务报表发表无法表示意见。当然，管理层的书面声明只是内部证据，总体而言，其证明力是非常有限的。管理层已提供可靠书面声明的事实，并不影响审计人员就管理层责任履行情况或具体认定获取的其他审计证据的性质和范围。

E－4 Audit Finalisation and the Final Review / 完成审计和最后的复核

Misstatement

Misstatement is a difference between the amount, classification, presentation, or disclosure of a reported financial statement item and the amount, classification, presentation, or disclosure that is required for the item to be in accordance with the applicable financial reporting framework. Misstatements can arise from error or fraud. When the auditor expresses an opinion on whether the financial statements are presented fairly, in all material respects, or give a true and fair view, misstatements also include those adjustments of amounts, classifications, presentation, or disclosures that, in the auditor's judgment, are necessary for the financial statements to be presented fairly, in all material respects, or to give a true and fair view.

错报

错报是指某一财务报表项目的金额、分类、列报或披露,与按照适用的财务报告编制基础应当列示的金额、分类、列报或披露之间存在的差异,或根据审计人员的判断,为使财务报表在所有重大方面实现公允反映,需要对金额、分类、列报或披露做出的必要调整。错报可能是由于错误或舞弊导致的。

Uncorrected Misstatements

Uncorrected misstatements are misstatements that the auditor has accumulated during the audit and that have not been corrected. To assist the auditor in evaluating the effect of misstatements accumulated during the audit and in communicating misstatements to management and those charged with governance, it may be useful to distinguish between factual misstatements, judgmental misstatements and projected misstatements.

Factual misstatements are misstatements about which there is no doubt.

Judgmental misstatements are differences arising from the judgments of management concerning accounting estimates that the auditor considers unreasonable, or the selection or application of accounting policies that the auditor considers inappropriate.

Projected misstatements are the auditor's best estimate of misstatements in populations, involving the projection of misstatements identified in audit samples to the entire populations from which the samples were drawn.

未更正错报

未更正错报是指审计人员在审计过程中累积的未更正的错报。为了帮助审计人员更好地评估审计过程中累积错报的影响，以及更好地与公司治理层沟通错报，需要区分事实错报、判断错报和推断错报。

事实错报是毋庸置疑的错报。比如，审计人员在审计中发现购入的固定资产的实际价值为 60 000 元，但被审计单位账面记录的金额为 69 000 元，则高估的 9 000 元就是对事实的错报。

判断错报是指审计人员认为管理层对会计估计做出不合理的判断或不恰当地选择和运用会计政策而导致的差异。其实质就是管理层对会计估计值的判断超出了审计人员确定的一个合理范围，或者审计人员不认可管理层选用的会计政策，从而产生的判断差异。

推断错报是指审计人员对总体存在的错报做出的最佳估计数，涉及根据在审计样本中识别出的错报来推断总体的错报。推断错报通常是指通过测试样本估计出总体的错报，再减去测试中发现的已经识别的具体错报。

【学习提示】

在审计完成阶段，如何评价审计过程中识别的累积错报？

根据审计准则，审计人员需要及时地

将审计过程中所有的累积错报与被审计单位的管理层进行沟通，然后被审计单位应该对财务报表做出相应的调整。如果管理层拒绝调整错报，就必须给出合理解释，审计才能据此判断财务报表是否不存在重大错报。在审计完成阶段，审计人员应当考虑财务报表中的未更正错报的汇总数是否重要。另外，审计人员还需要将所有未更正错报以及影响，与被审计单位的治理层进行沟通。并且，准则要求被审计单位的管理层和治理层应当提供一份书面声明给审计人员，声明他们确信未更正错报（无论是单个还是汇总）是不重要的。

E-5 Audit Report / 审计报告

Audit Report

The audit report communicates the auditor's findings to users. The objectives of the auditor are:

(a) To form an opinion on the financial statements based on an evaluation of the conclusions drawn from the audit evidence obtained; and

(b) To express clearly that opinion through a written report.

The audit report contains the following elements:

(a) Title;

(b) Addressee;

(c) Auditor's opinion;

(d) Basis for opinion;

(e) Key audit matters (for listed entities);

(f) Responsibilities of management and those charged with governance for the financial statements;

(g) Auditor's responsibilities for the audit of the financial statements;

(h) Report on other legal and regulatory requirements;

(i) Name of the engagement partner;

(j) Signature of the auditor;

(k) Auditor's address;

(l) Date of the auditor's report.

审计报告

审计报告将审计人员的发现传达给其使用者。审计报告的目的是：

1. 根据评估所获得的审计证据得出的结论，形成对财务报表的意见；

2. 通过书面报告明确地表达意见。

审计报告包括下列要素：

1. 标题；

2. 收件人；

3. 审计意见；

4. 形成审计意见的基础；

5. 关键审计事项（对上市公司的要求）；

6. 管理层和治理层对财务报表的责任；

7. 审计人员对财务报表审计的责任；

8. 按照相关法律法规的要求报告的事项（如适用）；

9. 审计人员的签名和盖章；

10. 会计师事务所的盖章；

11. 会计师事务所的地址；

12. 审计报告的日期。

Unmodified Opinion

The unmodified opinion is the opinion expressed by the auditor when the auditor concludes that the financial statements are prepared, in all material respects, in accordance with the applicable financial reporting framework.

无保留意见

无保留意见是指当审计人员认为财务报表在所有重大方面按照适用的财务报告编制基础编制并实现公允反映时发表的审计意见。

Modified Opinion

The modified opinion includes a qualified opinion, an adverse opinion and a disclaimer of opinion.

Qualified Opinion

The auditor shall express a qualified opinion when:

(a) The auditor, having obtained sufficient appropriate audit evidence, concludes that misstatements, individually or in the aggregate, are material, but not pervasive, to the financial statements; or

(b) The auditor is unable to obtain sufficient appropriate audit evidence on which to base the opinion, but the auditor concludes that the possible effects on the financial statements of undetected misstatements, if any, could be material but not pervasive.

Adverse Opinion

The auditor shall express an adverse opinion when the

auditor, having obtained sufficient appropriate audit evidence, concludes that misstatements, individually or in the aggregate, are both material and pervasive to the financial statements.

Disclaimer of Opinion

The auditor shall disclaim an opinion when the auditor is unable to obtain sufficient appropriate audit evidence on which to base the opinion, and the auditor concludes that the possible effects on the financial statements of undetected misstatements, if any, could be both material and pervasive.

The auditor shall disclaim an opinion when, in extremely rare circumstances involving multiple uncertainties, the auditor concludes that, notwithstanding having obtained sufficient appropriate audit evidence regarding each of the individual uncertainties, it is not possible to form an opinion on the financial statements due to the potential interaction of the uncertainties and their possible cumulative effect on the financial statements.

非无保留意见

非无保留意见包括保留意见、否定意见和无法表示意见。

保留意见

当存在下列情形之一时，审计人员应当发表保留意见：

1. 审计人员在获取充分、适当的审计证据后，认为错报单独或汇总起来对财务报表影响重大，但不具有广泛性。

2. 审计人员无法获取充分、适当的审计证据以形成审计意见，但认为如有未发现的错报，其对财务报表可能产生的影响虽然重大，却不具有广泛性。

否定意见

审计人员在获取充分、适当的审计证据后，如果认为错报单独或汇总起来对财务报表的影响重大且具有广泛性，审计人员应当发表否定意见。

无法表示意见

如果审计人员无法获取充分、适当的审计证据以形成审计意见，并且认为如有未发现错报，其对财务报表可能产生的影响重大且具有广泛性，这时应当发表无法表示意见。

在极少数情况下，可能存在多个不确定事项。尽管审计人员对每个单独的不确定事项获取了充分、适当的审计证据，但由于不确定事项之间可能存在相互影响，以及可能对财务报表产生累积影响，审计人员不可能对财务报表形成审计意见。在这种情况下，审计人员应当发表无法表示意见。

【学习提示】

如何确定审计意见的类型？

审计人员在确定恰当的审计意见类型时，主要考虑两个因素：一是财务报表是否存在重大错报；二是审计人员是否能够获取充分、适当的审计证据。

如果审计人员能够获取充分适当的审计证据，认为财务报表不存在重大错报，则应当发表无保留意见。如果审计人员获取充分适当的证据，认为财务报表有重大错报，这时，再根据错报的程度应发表保留意见或否定意见。错报重大但不具有广泛性，则发表保留意见；错报重大且具有广泛性，则发表否定意见。

如果审计人员无法获取充分适当的证据，也就是审计范围受到一定程度的限制，审计人员无法验证某些项目，则应根据受到限制的程度发表保留意见或无法表示意见。如果无法验证的项目重大但不具有广泛性，则发表保留意见；如果无法验证的项目重大且具有广泛性，则发表无法表示意见。

这就好比我们观察一个苹果，如果我们清楚地看到这个苹果有一部分已经腐烂，但是剔除这个腐烂的部分，苹果仍然可以食用，则发表保留意见；如果这个苹果已经完全变质，无法食用，则发表否定意见。当这个苹果被包装起来，有一部分我们无法观察到，但就可以观察到的部分来看，苹果仍可以食用，则发表保留意见；如果包装特别严密，我们完全无法确定苹果的好坏，则发表无法表示意见。

Key Audit Matters

Key audit matters are those matters that, in the auditor's professional judgment, were of most significance in the audit of the financial statements of the current period. Key audit matters are selected from matters communicated with those charged with governance.

关键审计事项

关键审计事项是指审计人员根据职业判断认为对本期财务报表审计最为重要的事项。关键审计事项从审计人员与治理层沟通过的事项中选取。

【学习提示】

关键审计事项到底是什么？

在审计报告中沟通关键审计事项是最新的审计报告准则的要求。在理解关键审计事项时，一定要把它们与那些导致非无保留意见的事项区分清楚。

如果某些事项导致审计人员应当发表非无保留意见，审计人员就不得在审计报告的关键审计事项部分沟通这些事项。另外要注意，可能导致对被审计单位持续经营能力产生重大疑虑的事项或情况存在重大不确定性，就其性质而言也属于关键审计事项。然而，这些事项也不得在审计报告的关键审计事项部分进行描述。审计人员应当按照适用的审计准则的规定报告这些事项，并在关键审计事项部分提及形成保留(否定)意见的基础部分或与持续经营相关的重大不确定性部分。

所以，我们可以把关键审计事项理解为对本期财务审计最为重要，且被审计单位根据会计准则已经对此进行了充分的披露(如果需要)的事项。审计人员在逐项描述关键审计事项时，应当分别索引至财务报表的相关披露(如有)，并同时说明下列内容：第一，该事项被认定为审计中最为重要的事项之一，因而被确定为关键审计事项的原因；第二，该事项在审计中是如何应对的。

可能需要沟通的关键审计事项主要包括：重大舞弊风险、商誉的确认和计量、金融工具的计价、新颁布的会计准则的影响，收入的确认等。

Pervasive

Pervasive is a term used, in the context of misstatements, to describe the effects on the financial statements of misstatements or the possible effects on the financial statements of misstatements, if any, that are undetected due to an inability to obtain sufficient appropriate audit evidence. Pervasive effects on the financial statements are those that, in the auditor's judgment:

(a) Are not confined to specific elements, accounts or

items of the financial statements;

(b) If so confined, represent or could represent a substantial proportion of the financial statements; or

(c) In relation to disclosures, are fundamental to users' understanding of the financial statements.

广泛性

广泛性，是描述错报影响的术语，用以说明错报对财务报表的影响，或者由于无法获取充分、适当的审计证据而未发现的错报(如存在)对财务报表可能产生的影响。根据审计人员的判断，对财务报表的影响具有广泛性的情形包括下列方面：

1. 不限于对财务报表的特定要素、账户或项目产生影响；

2. 虽然仅对财务报表的特定要素、账户或项目产生影响，但这些要素、账户或项目是或可能是财务报表的主要组成部分；

3. 当与披露相关时，产生的影响对财务报表使用者理解财务报表至关重要。

【学习提示】

如何理解"广泛性"这个概念?

上述"广泛性"的定义中，所谓"不限于对财务报表特定要素、账户或项目产生影响"的情形，是指财务报表中多个项目产生重大错报。比如，应收账款项目未计提坏账准备，导致该项目被严重高估；长期股权投资的核算方法不正确，导致该项目被严重高估；应付账款项目被严重低估。所有错报都是重要的，而且被错报的余额对企业财务状况有特别重大的影响。

上述定义中的第二种情形是指财务报表中某个主要项目出现

特别重大错报。比如，被审计单位将自建的用于出售的房屋全部列示为“固定资产”而非“存货”，且该项资产占到资产总额的80%。这时，该项错报就是具有广泛性的错报。

上述第三种情形是指对理解财务报表有重大影响的需要披露的事项。比如，有关被审计单位的持续经营存在重大的不确定性，而被审计单位拒绝披露。这项具有广泛性的错报可能导致审计人员发表否定意见。

理解“广泛性”这个概念，是发表恰当的审计意见的基础。与“重要性”一样，这也取决于审计人员的专业判断。导致发表非无保留意见的事项对财务报表的影响重大但不具有广泛性时，审计人员应当发表保留意见；当该事项对财务报表的影响是重大且具有广泛性时，审计人员根据该事项的性质发表否定意见（财务报表有重大错报），或无法表示意见（无法获取充分、适当的审计证据）。

Emphasis of Matter Paragraph

The emphasis of matter paragraph is a paragraph included in the auditor's report that refers to a matter appropriately presented or disclosed in the financial statements that, in the auditor's judgment, is of such importance that it is fundamental to users' understanding of the financial statements.

强调事项段

强调事项段，是指审计报告中含有的一个段落，该段落提及已在财务报表中恰当列报或披露的事项，且根据审计人员的职业判断，该事项对财务报表使用者理解财务报表至关重要。

Other Matter Paragraph

The other matter paragraph is a paragraph included in the auditor's report that refers to a matter other than those presented or disclosed in the financial statements that, in the auditor's judgment, is relevant to users' understanding of the audit, the auditor's responsibilities or the auditor's report.

其他事项段

其他事项段，是指审计报告中含有的一个段落，该段落提及未在财务报表中列报或披露的事项，且根据审计人员的职业判断，该事项与财务报表使用者理解审计工作、审计人员的责任或审计报告相关。

【学习提示】

如何区分强调事项与其他事项？

强调事项主要用于强调被审计单位已在财务报表中列报或披露，但是审计人员认为这些事项对财务报表使用者理解财务报表至关重要，所以强调事项往往需要明确提及被强调事项以及相关披露在财务报表的位置，强调事项段常用“如财务报表附注×所述”的字样引出。需要增加强调事项的情形主要包括：在允许的情况下提前应用对财务报表有广泛影响的新会计准则；或者存在已经或持续对被审计单位财务状况产生重大影响的特大灾难等。

这里需要特别关注有关“持续经营”的披露问题。根据最新的审计报告准则，如果审计人员认为被审计单位运用持续经营假设是适当的，但存在重大不确定性，且财务报表对重大不确定性已做出充分披露，这时审计人员应当在审计报告中增加以“与持续经营相关的重大不确定性”为标题的单独部分，以提醒财务报表使用者关注这些事项或情况，不需要在强调事项段中说明。

而其他事项主要用于沟通那些未在财务报表中列报或披露，但是审计人员认为这些事项与财务报表使用者理解审计工作、审计人员的责任或审计报告相关，比如前期财务报表由其他会计师事务所审计等事项。

需要注意，不论是强调事项还是其他事项，都不包括导致审计人员发表非无保留意见的事项，以及被确定为在审计报告中沟通的关键审计事项。

Comparative Information

The comparative information refers to the amounts and disclosures included in the financial statements in respect of one or more prior periods in accordance with the applicable financial reporting framework.

比较信息

比较信息，是指包含于财务报表中的、符合适用的财务报告编制基础的，与一个或多个以前期间相关的金额和披露。

Corresponding Figures

Corresponding Figures — Comparative information where amounts and other disclosures for the prior period are included as an integral part of the current period financial statements, and are intended to be read only in relation to the amounts and other disclosures relating to the current period (referred to as “current period figures”). The level of detail presented in the corresponding amounts and disclosures is dictated primarily by its relevance to the current period figures.

对应数据

对应数据属于比较信息，是指作为本期财务报表组成部分的上期金额和相关披露，这些金额和披露只能和与本期相关的金额和披露（称为"本期数据"）联系起来阅读。对应数据列报的详细程度主要取决于其与本期数据的相关程度。

Comparative Financial Statements

Comparative Financial Statements — Comparative information where amounts and other disclosures for the prior period are included for comparison with the financial statements of the current period but, if audited, are referred to in the auditor's opinion. The level of information included in those comparative financial statements is comparable with that of the financial statements of the current period.

比较财务报表

比较财务报表属于比较信息，是指为了与本期财务报表相比较而包含的上期金额和相关披露。如果上期金额和相关披露已经审计，就会在审计意见中提及。比较财务报表包含信息的详细程度与本期财务报表包含信息的详细程度相似。

【学习提示】

比较财务信息是如何影响审计报告的？

审计人员之所以关注比较财务信息，是因为会计准则对比较

信息的列报提出了要求，比较信息是当期财务报表不可缺少的组成部分。

提示：我们学习的重点是比较信息对审计报告的影响。

当财务报表中列报对应数据时，由于对应数据是本期数据的组成部分，审计意见是针对包括对应数据的本期财务报表整体的，审计意见通常不提及对应数据。比如，资产负债表中“应收账款”项目的期末余额，由上期财务报表中“应收账款”项目的期末余额加上本期增加金额减去本期减少金额得出，因而不需要再单独提及上期的“应收账款”项目。除非上期的“应收账款”项目存在重大错报，而该财务报表未经更正，并且本期也未对期初应收账款进行恰当重述。这时审计人员应当在审计报告中提及对应数据。在“形成保留意见(或否定意见)的基础”中，解释上期应收账款的错报及其对上期和本期财务报表的影响。

当列报比较财务报表时，由于比较财务报表出具的审计报告涵盖所列报的每期财务报表，审计人员的审计意见应当提及列报的财务报表所属的各期，以及发表的审计意见涵盖的各期。比如，在列报 20×6 年的财务报表时，根据会计准则可能还需要列报 20×5 年和 20×4 年的财务报表作为比较。审计人员的审计范围包括三个会计年度，而其审计意见也必须分别针对这三个会计年度。这时，就可能出现审计人员对 20×4 年和 20×5 年的财务报表发表无保留意见，而对 20×6 年的财务报表发表保留意见的情形。

Other Information

The other information refers to the financial or non-financial information (other than financial statements and the auditor's report thereon) included in an entity's annual report.

其他信息

其他信息是指在被审计单位年度报告中包含的除财务报表和审计报告以外的财务信息和非财务信息。

Annual Report

The annual report is a document, or combination of documents, prepared typically on an annual basis by management or those charged with governance in accordance with law, regulation or custom, the purpose of which is to provide owners (or similar stakeholders) with information on the entity's operations and the entity's financial results and financial position as set out in the financial statements. An annual report contains or accompanies the financial statements and the auditor's report thereon and usually includes information about the entity's developments, its future outlook and risks and uncertainties, a statement by the entity's governing body, and reports covering governance matters.

年度报告

年度报告，是指管理层或治理层根据法律法规的规定或惯例，一般以年度为基础编制的、旨在向所有者(或类似的利益相关方)提供实体经营情况和财务业绩及财务状况(财务业绩及财务状况反映于财务报表)信息的一份文件或系列文件组合。一份年度报告包含或随附财务报表和审计报告，通常包括实体的发展，未来的前景、风险和不确定事项，治理层声明，以及包含治理事项的报告等信息。

Misstatement of the Other Information

A misstatement of the other information exists when the other information is incorrectly stated or otherwise misleading (including because it omits or obscures information necessary for a proper understanding of a matter disclosed in the other information).

其他信息的错报

其他信息的错报，是指对其他信息做出不正确陈述或其他信息具有误导性，包括遗漏或掩饰对恰当理解其他信息披露的事项必要的信息。

【学习提示】

1. 审计人员为什么需要关注年度报告中的其他信息？

其他信息可能包括：管理层或治理层的经营报告；财务数据摘要；员工情况数据；财务比率；董事和高级管理人员的姓名；等等。

审计人员没有专门责任确定其他信息是否得到适当陈述。审计人员的目标是，在已经阅读其他信息的情况下，考虑其他信息与财务报表之间是否存在重大不一致。重大不一致可能导致审计人员对依据以前获取的审计证据得出的审计结论产生怀疑，甚至对形成审计意见的基础产生怀疑。另外，在阅读其他财务信息以识别重大不一致时，审计人员可能会注意到明显的对事实的重大错报。对事实的重大错报可能损害含有已审计财务报表的文件的可信性。审计人员需要关注这些错报对审计报告可能的影响。

如果在审计报告日前获取的其他信息中识别出重大不一致，并且需要对已审计财务报表做出修改，但管理层拒绝做出修改，审计人员应当在审计报告中发表非无保留意见。如果审计人员识别出重大不一致或对事实的重大错报，需要修改其他信息，但管理层拒绝修改，那么审计人员应当与管理层讨论，并且将对其他信息的疑虑告知治理层，进而采取适当的进一步措施。

2. 审计报告是如何分类的？

审计报告可以分为两大类：标准格式审计报告和非标准格式审计报告。标准格式审计报告即标准的无保留意见的审计报告。非无保留审计意见的审计报告属于非标准格式审计报告。除此以外，如果审计人员已经获取充分、适当的审计证据，认为被审计单位的财务报表是真实、公允的，但是有一些额外的信息需要沟通，就可以根据具体情况使用强调事项段、其他事项段，或者增加"与持续经营相关的重大不确定性"的部分。这样的审计报告属于非标准格式审计报告。对审计报告的分类见下图：

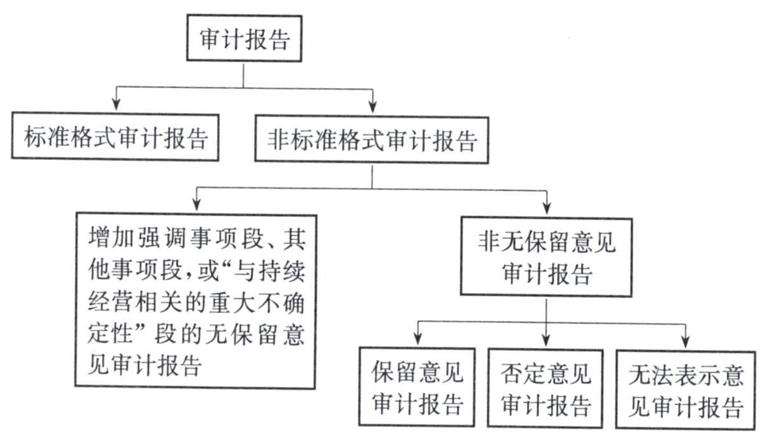